CW01221136

Moments *of* Love
An eight-day retreat with the Song of Songs

JOHN MANN

DARTON·LONGMAN+TODD
INTELLIGENT ♦ INSPIRATIONAL ♦ INCLUSIVE
SPIRITUAL BOOKS

By the same author:
Lent with Saint John's Gospel
Journeying to the Light
Christ's Seven Words from the Cross

and forthcoming in 2025
Be still, be silent: Reflections on the poetry of David Scott

First published in 2025 by
Darton, Longman and Todd Ltd
Unit 1, The Exchange
6 Scarbrook Road
Croydon CR0 1UH
editorial@darton-longman-todd.co.uk

This product conforms to the requirements of the European Union's General Product Safety Regulations (GPSR).
EU Authorised Representative for GPSR:
Easy Access System Europe –
Mustamäe tee 50, 10621 Tallinn, Estonia
gpsr.requests@easproject.com

© 2025 John Mann

The right of John Mann to be identified as the Author of this work has been asserted in accordance with the Copyright, Designs and Patents Act 1988.

ISBN: 978-1-917362-00-9

Scripture quotations are from New Revised Standard Version Bible: Anglicized Edition, copyright © 1989, 1995 National Council of the Churches of Christ in the United States of America. Used by permission. All rights reserved worldwide.

Acknowledgements: Denise Levertov, *New Selected Poems* (Bloodaxe Books, 2003). Reproduced with permission of Bloodaxe Books.
www.bloodaxebooks.com
@bloodaxebooks (twitter/facebook) #bloodaxebooks

Cover image: Shulamite Bride © Lisa Van der Plas. Used by kind permission.

A catalogue record for this book is available from the British Library.

Printed and bound in Great Britain by Short Run Press, Exeter

Contents

Acknowledgements	4
Foreword by Bishop Michael Burrows	6
Introduction	9
Day 1 Welcome	13
Day 2 Acceptance	31
Day 3 The Quest	49
Day 4 Beauty	65
Day 5 The Wound of Love	81
Day 6 Seeing	99
Day 7 The Invitation of Love	115
Day 8 Consummation	129

Acknowledgements

THE PREPARATION OF this book has only been possible with the help of a number of people who have helped through the stages of writing, submission, design, permissions and final production. Thanks especially to my wife Helen whose questions, observations, support and encouragement and proof reading have been essential. To Michael Burrows, who so willingly agreed to write the foreword, I am truly grateful. The staff at DLT, especially David Moloney, Helen Porter and Judy Linard for their advice, design and guidance, and to all who have shown patience and help, particularly Suzanne Fairless-Aitken, rights and permissions officer at Bloodaxe Books.

Formally, I add recognition of the importance to this publication of all the quotations, whether requiring actual permission or not, with personal thanks:

First Love by Denise Levertov from *New Selected Poems* (Bloodaxe Books, 2003), reproduced with permission of Bloodaxe Books. www.bloodaxebooks.com @bloodaxebooks (twitter/facebook) #bloodaxebooks

Scripture quotations are from New Revised Standard Version Bible: Anglicized Edition, copyright © 1989, 1995 National Council of the Churches of Christ in the United States of America. Used by permission. All rights reserved worldwide.

Acknowledgements

To the Paulist Press for allowing use of Kieran Kavanaugh's translation of selected lines of the *Spiritual Canticle* of St John of the Cross.

With particular gratitude I acknowledge the permission of Lisa Van der Plas for use of her Shulamite Bride painting on the cover of the book. Linked specifically to the end of chapter 6 of the Song of Songs, with the dance of the Shulamite Bride suggestive of peace and reconciliation in derivation and action, I am delighted to have such a cover picture.

Dedication

INSPIRATION AND CREATIVITY flowing from love experienced between individuals or, indeed, within oneself, produce works and emotions that themselves generate opportunities for qualities also recognised as gifts of the Holy Spirit. A conscious awareness of the power of love opens a window through which we are open to God. At least two examples appear in this book, with Lisa Van der Plas' painting used for the cover being inspired by her daughter Noa Eden, and Denise Levertov's *First Love*, being, in fact, her first consciousness of love.

I dedicate this book to all whose lives are being or have been touched by the Love of God in Christ Jesus, and whose response has led to the transforming effects of love and the inspiration of the Holy Spirit being experienced by others, bringing healing, reconciliation, forgiveness and renewal.

Foreword

by Bishop Michael Burrows

MOST OF US, to be frank, approach the Song of Songs with a blend of trepidation and confusion. The prospect of spending an hour with it, let alone a concentrated week, is enough to send us running, almost Jonah-like, in the opposite direction.

So many things scare us … we cannot cope with the imagery, the explicitly erotic content is just too much, we cannot make head or tail of how it might best be allegorised, and in truth we really do not grasp what it is about at all or how it managed to find its way into the canon.

In this wonderfully imaginative little book, John Mann liberates us from all our fears. With truly inspired literary alchemy, he turns our nightmares about the Song into the most beautiful dreams and restores to our understanding of the text that loveliness which should be its most obvious attribute.

Thus we are invited, in a structured manner which, while demanding, still offers ample scope for reflection, meditation, exercise and sleep, to let the text wash over us in the course of an eight-day retreat. We are drawn into the mystery of lover, beloved and their mutual love … the most explicit words and daring images somehow become balm-soaked gateways to enhancing our intimacy with Christ, not least in the setting of the Eucharist. We realise the pathway is not always easy, for true love demands times when there are shadows, disappointments and absences. Yet we never fear to dream on, knowing that we are promised an awakening into a place where beauty is cherished and where the spiritual life is fragrant. The capacity of John's book, like the Song itself, to appeal to all the senses is quite remarkable. It may be written on paper, but one occasionally raises one's head from the pages truly experiencing perfume, and glimpsing the utter beauty of the plants and the animals which inhabit the garden of delights where the pursuit of love is played out. And that pursuit is carried out with an unapologetic intensity which is thoroughly refreshing.

For all its insight and learning (and regarding the latter just glance at the evidence provided by the allusions and footnotes), this is a book written with modesty. The author keeps his distance behind the poetry which he is generously illuminating. But, that said, those of us who know John Mann know full well that these words and this approach to a supremely challenging text could only be his. He writes with the eye and the spirit of the true mystic; indeed the great mystics of yore whose words he readily quotes seem like his own friends. His inspiration moves frequently and naturally from the altar to the garden, and in the latter context each plant and flower seems to know him. He walks companionably, indeed romantically, with his wife Helen amid the Manx glens which now embrace their island home, and as they look in different directions and spot different things, there is nevertheless a wholeness of perspective befitting two individuals who have long walked and loved together. Thus John writes not only academically but experientially in his response to the Song. Interestingly, while this little book is aimed largely at the solo Christian on retreat, it will send him or her back from the imaginative garden of delights to the wondrous garden of real relationships, where we all know that in our quest for intimacy with Christ we who seek his healing and wholeness will forever need to journey hand in hand with other loved ones in order to be whole ourselves.

Please take the time this book requires in order to benefit truly from it. Savour its words and do not think they should be digested hastily. Enjoy its somewhat daring ingredients but also be grateful for its gentleness. Allow it to feed your dreams, your delights, your walks, your musings, your own songs. It is a joy for me to commend this work by a priest of great integrity who writes as he lives, whose ministry has always been characterised by an unswerving quest for truth, beauty and healing, and for whose genuinely fragrant spirituality his admirers remain grateful.

Michael Burrows
Bishop of Tuam, Limerick and Killaloe
October 2024

Introduction

I HAVE LONG had it in mind to write a book on the Song of Songs. It is a work that is familiar because of a small number of well-known passages, its rather scandalous reputation for eroticism and its design, which is entirely allegorical. Why it is loved is because it deals so directly with the subject of desire that those whose love of the poetic is finely tuned, find within it a close and beautiful expression of the essence of devotion to God. The Christian has no difficulty in accepting this with the fullness of adoration of Christ in the mystical unity of the Church. Female and male, in this understanding, become interchangeable in the allegory, and so the fluidity of the gender relationships is another way of adapting the work to the extraordinarily complex nature of human identity as we enter the second quarter of the twenty-first century.

The fact that this reasoning will, in all likelihood, find critical opinions from every shade of theological understanding adds a frisson to the attempt to unravel the beauty, but, hopefully, lose not the underlying sense of awe and wonder in the very nature of love, both human and divine. What encourages me to read once more the verses of this book and tease out the meaning is the quality of minds that have troubled their hearts with homilies and commentaries on it from the past, including Origen, Gregory of Nyssa and Gregory the Great in the early Christian centuries, with the Cistercians Bernard of Clairvaux, and William of Thierry[1] half a millennia later, and, later again, with a burning flame of mystical love, St John of the Cross. It is to his *A Spiritual Canticle of the Soul* that I turn, with both his poetry and his commentary as the supplementary inspiration for my attempt at weaving the themes of the Song of Songs into a reflective whole.

What form the book was to take was a factor that has held me up for some time, but I have settled on leading an eight day retreat, which may be used by the reader at home or away, whilst in the full busyness of ordinary life, with four significant pauses a day, or in the quiet and peace of a place set aside for retreat and with no other thoughts or pressures to cloud the mind of thought on the words of these few chapters.[2] This book is unlikely to be read by anyone other than those drawn to allegory, but accepting that the poetic lies at the centre of most of our hearts, I am inclined to think that that is many of us. The scandal, if such there be in texts that are so obviously filled with human desire and physical awareness of beauty in attracting the most intimate of unions, is quickly dispelled in

---

[1] Origen, 'The Song of Songs'.; Gregory of Nyssa, 'Homily on the Song of Songs'; Gregory the Great, 'On the Song of Songs'; Bernard of Clairvaux, 'Sermons on the Song of Songs'; William of Thierry, 'Exposition on the Song of Songs'.

[2] With thirty-two sections, four for each day of eight, it is adaptable for use over a month, with one reflection a day, whilst ignoring the references to the time of day.

Day 1

the counter-claim of how we declare and express perfect love, and understand its veiled presence in a number of instances in the Scriptures. From the woman who anointed Christ and wiped the excess perfumed oil from his body with her hair, to John who lay close to our Lord at the Last Supper; from Mary and the other women at the foot of the cross and those preparing Christ's body for burial, to recalling the tenderness of earlier examples of loving attention from Ruth and Naomi, through to David and Jonathan, and onwards to the very understanding of Joseph and Mary approaching the birth of their first-born son Jesus, the gentle and committed attention of Anna and Simeon for the infant Christ and the devotion of Mary and Martha in welcoming our Lord within their home at Bethany.

The Song of Songs, relates nothing of any of these particular examples of intimate feelings between human beings. In the desire of one individual for God, within the divinely-ordained society which is the Body of Christ, we are frequently holding biblical associations of individuals in our minds as we relate one to another. However, there is inevitably a subconscious awareness of reading them all in; including them all at the periphery of our thoughts, if you like, and drawing on their expressions of love. So we relate their experience, as we read of them in the Scriptures, to our relationship with God. As we do this, we are in tune with the writer of the Song of Songs.

The Song of Songs inspires by touching us where we are vulnerable and causing an emotional as well as a devotional response, even reducing us to tears. I risk the accusation of submitting to fantasy by holding my faith in the unconscious, or at least unconscionable, transference of meaning from picture to reality that relies on the power of metaphor to exceed that of plain description. Whether I have succeeded in this I leave the reader to decide. The text I am using throughout is the NRSV. This is not a critical commentary on the book, so I am ignoring the difficulty of some questions of translation which have little, if any, bearing on the overall theme, and would interrupt the flow of the narrative.

DAY 1
Welcome

DAY 1
Morning

Song of Songs 1:1-4

> *The Song of Songs, which is Solomon's.*
>
> *Let him kiss me with the kisses of his mouth!*
> *For your love is better than wine,*
> *your anointing oils are fragrant,*
> *your name is perfume poured out;*
> *therefore the maidens love you.*
> *Draw me after you, let us make haste.*
> *The king has brought me into his chambers.*
> *We will exult and rejoice in you;*
> *we will extol your love more than wine;*
> *rightly do they love you.*

SONGS, EFFECTIVELY POETRY set to music, are part of the cultural identity of individuals and nations. Whether standing hand on heart for an anthem in pride and confidence, or kneeling, prostrate with tears of anguish as words and music rifle through our innards, teasingly reminding us of sorrow or pain. Whether a song puts a smile on our faces or a grimace reflecting something deeply challenging to us, there is no doubting the effect on nearly all humanity of the power of song to move – and catch us unawares

Moments of Love

with something of life below the superficial.

That the Song of Songs is Solomon's is the claim of verse 1. The very opening of the book claims kingship for its author, and Solomon it is. Well, maybe it is, but in a more relevant meaning for today it is not so much Solomon's as yours and mine, or it can be, if the words resonate with the feelings that we may or may not keep hidden in those recesses of our lives, from days, months, years, even decades in the past. It is a comforting thought that they may be Solomon's words, for wisdom is associated with the King of Israel of that name, and wisdom is what we are seeking in these worrying days of the twenty-first century, be it because of war or climate change, poverty, disease or abuse, be it devotionally of the spirit or mentally of the intellect, we seek wisdom.

The Song cuts immediately to the quick: 'O that you would kiss me with the kisses of your mouth.' How we read this is critical to our understanding of the whole poem. Traditionally, the interpretation of the Song resides in the readers feeling his or her way to God, and for the Christian that is almighty God as incarnate in Christ. The kiss of the lover is the expression of intimacy that leaves its mark, unseen physically, but emotionally it is as tender a mark as the physical occurrences on Mount Sinai: commandments cast in stone, the face of Moses shining with the presence of God, or with Elijah, the wrap of a mantle to shield one's inadequacy from the sight of what is beyond us.

We may take this as a gasp for revelation, whatever that revelation may cause to effect. St John of the Cross put it very starkly in Stanza xi of his *A Spiritual Canticle of the Soul*:

Day 1

Reveal Thy presence,
And let the vision and Thy beauty kill me.
Behold, the malady
Of love is incurable
Except in Thy presence and before Thy face.[3]

As Moses could see only the train of God, and Elijah experienced the presence of God in silence, so the opening of the Song of Songs is a sudden and unexpected shock, placing us instantly on tenterhooks. There is an edginess – far from comfortable complacency – in seeking what we do.

The lover's kiss holds us there and for those whose past holds relationships so special that moments of intimacy are still recalled with a greeting or parting kiss, or that first kiss of one's adored life's love. Here we are already entering the desired realm of this retreat. Fewer than twenty words of the Song, not the eight hundred or so of this morning's reflection, and the kiss, to which we shall return, has brought our desire for Christ to the place where the heart seeks confirmation and renewal.

Love is better than wine, and other adjuncts to intimate relationship, fragrant oils, loving attendants, comfortable and cosy rooms, words of exultation and rejoicing. This is how we settle this first hour of the retreat to the stilling of the heart in comfort, peace and joy. There is no better way to open the door of one's heart, and take the thought of the next seven days in the hope that this is going to be a time to wander in the

---

[3] *A Spiritual Canticle of the Soul*, St John of the Cross (London: Thomas Baker, 1919), p. 76.

paths that challenge gently and lead positively to the place of faith, hope and love. There is a Song to sing, and the voice is calling us to join its melody and find our own voice with the harmony of Christian fellowship and the company of the angelic beings, who live and worship in the view of the Almighty and the presence of the saints in light. Here is our opening, with Moses, Elijah and St John of the Cross, let us rejoice in it.

PRAYER

Heavenly Father,
as I begin this retreat,
have mercy on my wandering ways,
teach me quiet and make me be still,
with the kiss of your Spirit,
and the embrace of your love,
in Christ your Son
Amen.

DAY 1
Midday

Song of Songs 1:5-7

> *I am black and beautiful,*
> *O daughters of Jerusalem,*
> *like the tents of Kedar,*
> *like the curtains of Solomon.*
> *Do not gaze at me because I am dark,*
> *because the sun has gazed on me.*
> *My mother's sons were angry with me;*
> *they made me keeper of the vineyards,*
> *but my own vineyard I have not kept!*
> *Tell me, you whom my soul loves,*
> *where you pasture your flock,*
> *where you make it lie down at noon;*
> *for why should I be like one who is veiled*
> *beside the flocks of your companions?*

I THINK THAT we can gather quite a picture of this young woman from these verses of delight in sunshine and rustic life. Life in the vineyard and the pastures, skin darkened in the sun's 'gaze'. Her brothers have put her to work, but her mind is on he who is loved, and on her own beauty. Her beauty is like the 'curtains of Solomon', which were, no doubt, glorious, but the outdoor life would have indicated relative poverty, unlike the

Moments of Love

wealthy, such as *one who is veiled* and kept out of the sun for the sake of pale-skinned beauty.

As we face the brazen confidence of this woman in her own lovely appearance, we feel her registering her healthy lifestyle beyond, and superior to, the conventional beauty of the privileged women of her day, and we are invited to take courage in our own self-worth. As far as this short retreat goes, we may find comfort or awkwardness in this, but let it sit, for the moment, in the eye of this young woman gazed on by the sun and happy in her open-air life. Let us picture the waving grasses of rich pasture and hear the bees working the vine flowers, feel the breeze on our face and the warm sun on bare arms, as we tend the vines and remove the weeds – be unveiled in the light of God's glory, and know ourselves gazed upon as we are.

We began the day in the full embrace and kiss as boldly we appeal to know the presence of Christ as we begin a few days of prayer and reflection, and now we are being invited to lie in gentle relaxation, as upon a summer's day, drowsy even – though there is no hint of drowsiness in the Song of Songs! No matter. We shall take our midday moment to consider in the words of the Manx poet T. E. Brown, *If thou couldest empty all thyself of self, like to a shell dishabited,*[4] envisaging a wide, sandy beach, as he no doubt did, with an empty shell sitting in glorious isolation upon it, just waiting to be filled in his imagination with new life, and lifted

---

[4] *The Collected Poems of T. E. Brown* (McMillan, 1900, reprinted Manx Museum and National Trust 1976), p. 82. The poem from which the quotation is taken is called *Indwelling*.

Day 1

on the tide, and swept into a fresh situation. Maybe rather, pondering with the Irish poet W. B. Yeats, and thinking of surrounding yourself with what comforts and inspires, you may see yourself, *stand on the roadway, or on the pavements grey*, and dream:

I will arise and go now, and go to Innisfree,
And a small cabin build there, of clay and wattles made;
Nine bean-rows will I have there, a hive for the honey-bee,
And live alone in the bee-loud glade.

And I shall have some peace there, for peace comes dropping slow,
Dropping from the veils of the morning to where the cricket sings;
There midnight's all a glimmer, and noon a purple glow,
And evening full of the linnet's wings.

I will arise and go now, for always night and day
I hear lake water lapping with low sounds by the shore;
While I stand on the roadway, or on the pavements grey,
I hear it in the deep heart's core.[5]

This languid moment in the middle of the day, whether it is raining outside, or a freezing cold January, let it be a moment of peace, serenity and rest, with the young woman of sun-kissed beauty and with the breeze cooling her from

[5] W. B. Yeats, *The Poems* (Everyman's Library 1992), p. 60. The poem is *The Lake Isle of Innisfree*.

the toil of the warm summer fields. An hour to lie back in a deckchair, close your eyes and relax.

PRAYER

Father,
this session may seem like
an effort to escape,
but really I am trying to re-find
what I have lost, or imagine
I have lost, though I know
that in you all things are ever-present
in Christ Jesus our Lord
Amen.

DAY 1
Evening

Song of Songs 1:8-11

> *If you do not know,*
> *O fairest among women,*
> *follow the tracks of the flock,*
> *and pasture your kids*
> *beside the shepherds' tents.*
>
> *I compare you, my love,*
> *to a mare among Pharaoh's chariots.*
> *Your cheeks are comely with ornaments,*
> *your neck with strings of jewels.*
> *We will make you ornaments of gold,*
> *studded with silver.*

PHYSICAL ATTRACTION AND sexual pleasure have been at the heart of the discomfort felt by some for the inclusion of the Song of Songs in the canon of the Scriptures. The subject of desire is one close to the spiritual fulfilment of the Christian who draws near to Christ and seeks revelation, but, as we found this morning, it can lead St John of the Cross to find in God's beauty too great a thing for him to live, and we know from the Scriptures that God would not reveal his face to Moses, however, we may wish to contemplate

Moments of Love

what cannot be physically apprehended.

So it is that desire has its detractors, for desire touches our weaknesses as well as our highest and most noble aspirations. With regard to this short retreat on the Song of Songs it will, inevitably, become a subject in which we shall immerse ourselves, for the book revolves around this theme. If our mind is stimulated by simile and allegorical interpretation, and we see it as part of what makes life mysterious and wonderful, then the teasing out of the theme of desire will cause us no discomfort, rather the very opposite. However, it will be more of a challenge to those of us who feel the liberty of such interpretation as problematic, even dangerous.

Our lives are rarely simple. There are many issues to face, and at times we have challenges that dominate us, such as shortage of money, family or neighbourly disputes, housing problems, worries about our health or the health of someone we love, and so on. On a more long-term consideration – a lifelong one – we deal with day-to-day challenges according to how we draw our boundaries over many aspects of daily living, outlook and commitments. These can be the so called 'red' lines that we will never cross without severe consequences. And then there are what we might term 'lines in the sand', that we draw and may re-draw according to our circumstances.

In the evening of this first day of retreat, as we recap, the message throughout the last few hours has been one of getting into the right state of mind, with a first burst of acknowledgement – and nothing better than the kiss to wake us and excite us to be positive in heart and intent. Then at lunchtime, that comforting, sinking into rest, as in a deckchair in the sun of a summer's day, and now

Day 1

we consider how desire will forward our retreat further. All of this is as a simile for the wrapping of ourselves in the presence of he who for us is the healer of our ills and restorer of our fallenness. The kiss is both a welcome and a symbol of love, whilst the blossoming health of the sun-gazed skin brings the warmth of affection and acceptance. Now before or after our evening meal, as we settle to the evening ahead, the opening image is of the pasturing of flocks, the finding of the track to secure a place of safety. The picture moves on to the adornment of the woman in the eyes of the lover. The jewels and the gold and silver that add to the natural beauty of the woman, already attractive with her rustic glow of health.

We may be feeling far from attractive at this moment and, besides, spending eight days on quiet and probably isolated retreat, we may not even have a mirror to check on our appearance – nor need we. This is not about appearing at our physical best before Christ. Whilst humanity looks on the outward manifestation of our person, God looks to the heart, and it is there that our treasures may be brought out. Fearlessly and without embarrassment and any sense of pride or sorrow, we gently reveal ourselves to Christ. Maybe it is with some kind of physical gesture that we can make the mental step of opening the jewel box of our heart and see if anything of worth lies within. This we do fearlessly: think back to the kiss; to the sun on our warm skin. Life before Christ is not condemnation, it is acceptance; not fault-finding, but gently revealing. How often did Jesus tease out the problem with someone who came to him? Many times. Let us consider just Nicodemus alone, and we have the darkness and the fear to embrace, with the message of new life too. We are not to feel guilty that we are not fit to be in Christ's vision. None of us is. So let us not have this first night in an agony of remorse or the emptiness of wasted opportunities.

We have the kiss and the welcome to add to this hour and form the context for this day, and the invitation to open and unburden ourselves. We have precious things in our hands. Maybe not a string of jewels or a beautiful ornament of silver and gold, but things of even greater worth: the thoughts, loves, memories and thanksgivings – yes, with negative emotions as well – but for this moment, hold out your hands, as if they contain a velvet cloth with every precious thing you possess and you are holding them before Christ who loves you, in a gesture of open-hearted joy and commendation knowing you are safe and at peace.

PRAYER

Lord God Almighty,
King of kings and Lord of lords,
in majesty I behold what I imagine you to be,
but as the jewels resplendent in these verses
　　from the Song,
adorn the neck of a woman of beauty, so
let my true self be open to you and gazed upon
in a way that gives me
confidence, that, for all my failings
there is something beautiful that you see within
that is your creation and my gift
in Christ I pray.
Amen.

DAY 1
Night

Song of Songs 1:12-17

> *While the king was on his couch,*
> *my nard gave forth its fragrance.*
> *My beloved is to me a bag of myrrh*
> *that lies between my breasts.*
> *My beloved is to me a cluster of henna blossoms*
> *in the vineyards of En-gedi.*
>
> *Ah, you are beautiful, my love;*
> *ah, you are beautiful;*
> *your eyes are doves.*
> *Ah, you are beautiful, my beloved,*
> *truly lovely.*
> *Our couch is green;*
> *the beams of our house are cedar,*
> *our rafters are pine.*

IT IS QUITE normal to feel very tired at the end of the first day of a retreat. At least, I have found it to be so. It seems to be part of the process of switching off and relaxing. Turning from a busy life, if that is your experience, will accentuate this experience. It is as if your body is saying, 'it's good that you are taking a break, now for a restoring of the cells that are strained and kept at fever-pitch

Moments of Love

most days – and sometimes at night too'. Peace. Perfect peace. Relaxation and no clock-watching. You have all the time you need.

Tonight's reading has a fragrance in almost every verse: spikenard, myrrh, henna, cedar and pine. If you have some hand cream or body butter with a lovely smell to hand, maybe you would like to use your sense of smell in this last reflection of the day, as you settle yourself to the time of rest and sleep.

Spikenard, the ointment of Mary that she used on Jesus (John 12: 3) was produced in India from a form of valerian, *Nardostachys jatamansi*. Henry Baker Tristram (1822-1902) in his *Natural History of the Bible* describes how the perfume was produced by drying the shaggy stem of the plant.[6]

Myrrh, is even more familiar from the Scriptures being one of the gifts to the infant Jesus from the Magi, and linked to the funeral rite. It was also mixed with other spices and with gum to form an anointing oil, and incense with a very fragrant aroma. This surely is the implication in this passage, described as contained within a bag, I imagine a small pouch or tiny sac at her breast.

Henna was used as a dye, but also as a beautiful floral gift, used in religious rites in India. In fact it is still used in a devotional way today and may be seen on Arab market stalls for sale. It is used in cosmetics also, as the dried leaves can colour skin, nails and hair. The blossoms growing at En-gedi, an oasis near the Dead Sea, also give both fragrance and colour in a barren landscape.

Cedar and pine form two fragrant timbers used in construction. There is something of

---

[6] pp. 484/5

Day 1

permanence and high quality about anything made from cedar wood. The beams of a house constructed of such timber would be strong and durable – and be scented. We are more familiar still with the fresh smell of pine. I have a cabin built of Latvian spruce, which whilst not technically the same as a pine, gives the cabin much the same aroma. It is the place of my writing and prayer, and I am relaxed in its scent and beauty.

So, let us end the day in the presence of fragrance. There are oils for sleep and there are oils for relaxation, so too for anointing and healing. In this spirit we lie down and sleep with the confidence and security of a loved one enclosed in the symbols of rest: flowers, words of commendation, the oil of gladness and the bed coverings of comfort, warmth and gentleness.

PRAYER

Father, we pray,
'before the ending of the day'
and know that peace which passes
our understanding, or can imagine
nothing of what it really means.
But, grant it to me this night,
that I may rest in peace and know
all whom I love are under your care
both now and always,
in the fellowship of the Holy Spirit,
and in the love of Christ.
Amen.

DAY 2
Acceptance

DAY 2
Morning

Song of Songs 2:1-7

*I am a rose of Sharon,
a lily of the valleys.*

*As a lily among brambles,
so is my love among maidens.*

*As an apple tree among the trees of the wood,
so is my beloved among young men.
With great delight I sat in his shadow,
and his fruit was sweet to my taste.
He brought me to the banqueting house,
and his intention towards me was love.
Sustain me with raisins,
refresh me with apples;
for I am faint with love.
O that his left hand were under my head,
and that his right hand embraced me!
I adjure you, O daughters of Jerusalem,
by the gazelles or the wild does:
do not stir up or awaken love
until it is ready!*

Moments of Love

WELL RESTED, I hope, we begin a second day of retreat with one of the more familiar passages of the Song of Songs. However, before we proceed today and think a little more about our desire for God and the wonder of the created world, and even look too closely at ourselves, let us read some words of Evelyn Underhill that remind us to stay our restless thoughts and make sure we do not become self-obsessed:

> *I believe in One God. We begin there; not with our own needs, desires, feelings or obligations. Were all these abolished, His independent splendour would remain, as the truth that gives meaning to the world.*[7]

These words from her *School of Charity*, or a suchlike corrective, could be found in similar form in numerous other places, and offered by many writers on the spiritual life. A retreat can be, in equal measure, an indulgence and a chance to rethink; a comfort and a recalibration; a restorative and a reinvigoration. So we approach a beautiful passage of the Song of Songs with eyes as open for its questions and headings for thought, as we are absorbed by its lyricism.

Nevertheless, it is with delight that we enjoy the lyricism, and the verses for our first reflection of the day are full of beautiful and alluring images, and to spend some moments with them is a joy. Let us begin with the flowers. Rose of Sharon is a garden plant that escapes and spreads, but that is not the shrub that fits this reading. The 'rose', or perhaps more

---

[7] *Lent with Evelyn Underhill* (Mowbrays, 1964), p. 22.

Day 2

correctly, the 'crocus' we are thinking here is simply that of the lily, as a blossom to be seen on the Sharon Plain which is part of the coastal region lying between the Mediterranean Sea and the Samarian Hills. This fertile plain stretches from the southern end of Mount Carmel in the north to close to Tel Aviv in the south. The lily is most likely the white lily *Lilium candidum,* such as is seen in association with the Virgin Mary in Christian art, and adorns the sanctuary at festivals in our Churches.

One freezing cold December, my wife and I left buckets of these incredibly beautiful lilies overnight for Christmas church flowers We left them in the church porch thinking that behind a heavy door they would be safe, and they would adorn the reredos behind the altar for Christmas Day. Such was the cold that night they were all destroyed and we spent part of the busy last days of Advent scouring the shops for a substitute. There is none. They are the perfect bloom for the occasion and in the author of the Song of Songs placing them in mind within a patch of brambles, there can be no greater contrast of beauty symbolic of perfect humanity united with the divine, with the invasive coils of brambles, thorns clinging to clothes and tearing at exposed skin. The contrast is similar with blackberries, one of our choicest of fruits come the autumn – I speak as one who has done battle with briars many a time, whilst enjoying bramble jelly made by my wife from blackberries we have picked from the lanes of our village.

In order to plant a small orchard I cleared brambles amongst the bracken and gorse of the wild part of our garden, wherein lies my writing

Moments of Love

cabin. The trees we planted are mostly apple, of various types, but it will be a while before we are sitting under their shade or enjoying much weight of fruit. Nevertheless, that cutting back of self-seeded holly, overgrown blackthorn and accompanying ivy, exposing the thousands of bluebells that have been there forever, and placing apple trees amongst them, helps me to appreciate the image that the writer is producing here, of sweetness and shade, fruitfulness and loveliness. From the lily among the brambles we move to the apple of the eye, and the love with which they are created and have their being.

These metaphors find their conclusion in the banquet that has the lover's banner or gaze to transform a festal meal into something intimate, with the sweetness of raisins and apple. Faint with love, the scene is such that anyone who has ever been in love, can hardly fail to encompass with thoughts and knowing feelings. There is longing, desire and a deep mutual understanding of when and where the time is right. The Christian brings the consequent allegorical interpretation to the Eucharist, which is a love feast in which we receive of Christ in a mystical manner, and share with each other in the broken bread and wine outpoured of the Kingdom of God. It unites us not only with Christ and each other but with the Church universal and eternal. These images are powerful, and we begin to understand, if it has been veiled before, how and why this Scripture is part of the canon and finds its place within the Wisdom literature of the Abrahamic faiths, and the stirring and awakening of love coming in due place and time within our devotional life.

Day 2

PRAYER

Father,
place in my heart the desire
for renewal and new life.
Fill me with the honesty
to look to the needs of others
and be a beacon of hope,
and neither a source of gloom
nor a person centred solely
on my own happiness.
Keep my eyes where they should rest
on Christ your Son, my Lord.
Amen.

DAY 2
Midday

Song of Songs 2:8-13a

The voice of my beloved!
Look, he comes,
leaping upon the mountains,
bounding over the hills.
My beloved is like a gazelle
or a young stag.
Look, there he stands
behind our wall,
gazing in at the windows,
looking through the lattice.
My beloved speaks and says to me:
'Arise, my love, my fair one,
and come away;
for now the winter is past,
the rain is over and gone.
The flowers appear on the earth;
the time of singing has come,
and the voice of the turtle-dove
is heard in our land.
The fig tree puts forth its figs,
and the vines are in blossom;
they give forth fragrance.

Day 2

WITHOUT SPECIFICALLY REFERENCING it in the reflection, we read the mention of the gazelle in our first passage from the Song of Songs today. Now we engage more closely with this image, and from the fields we are transported to the mountains. Taking the interwoven pictures that the author conjures up in almost every passage of the book, this slow consideration of the text over eight concentrated days is seen and felt to be eye-opening; it absorbs a desire for colour, and adds texture to the images that seek to teach us something more of the truth of Christ's abiding love and acceptance for his fallen and broken sisters and brothers. We are lifted by the gazelle upon the mountains because it reflects freedom, life, energy and the hill-top where the air is rarified and fresh, and from which we gaze upon creation with clear sight.

The image doesn't cease here, rather it flows directly into another form, as the timid look of the deer, fearful of detection, gazing in stillness from behind a wall, glancing through the lattice. This is another scene capturing the devotional mood of one who has been touched with the love of God, but hardly knows how to deal with the emotion, so carried away with the conviction of forgiveness and of a reconciled and peaceful heart and mind. Are we receptive to the voice of Christ at this moment? Of course, as at no other time are we brought to know the reality, described in Julian of Norwich's words, 'All is well, and all manner of things are well'.

> *My beloved speaks and says to me:*
> *'Arise, my love, my fair one, and come away.'*

This call comes as our midday reflection unfolds with multiple metaphors, and considerable emotional energy. If our receptivity is great at this moment, then proceeding to unpick the call to still greater intimacy is the one that we can follow in heart and mind as the afternoon proceeds, but it may be that we are not at that 'due time and place' of which we thought earlier this morning. The love of God is constant and ever present, but our receptivity is far from steady, and depends on so many factors – tiredness and distraction amongst them – and maybe the coldness of experiencing the loss of the inspiration we once had. Concerns may be crowding in and we cannot simply dismiss them at will. So let us be circumspect, expectant and hopeful, but not be disheartened if at this moment we cannot feel able to *stir up or awaken love*. The disadvantage of becoming a hermit for eight days, and having no sounding board for spiritual direction to hand, leaves us needing to accept and live with the knowledge that imperfect feelings and tiredness and fragility are part of the reason why we are here and we must rest happily with that acceptance and knowledge, put any agitation or expectation to one side, and be at peace within ourselves.

So, actively entering in, or vicariously interested, but not experiencing any depth of feeling at this moment, let us consider how St John of the Cross imagined the 'words' of Christ to find their way within:

> *Oh flame of love so living,*
> *How tenderly you force*
> *To my soul's inmost core your fiery probe!*
> *Since now you've no misgiving,*

Day 2

*End it, pursue your course
And for our sweet encounter tear the robe!*[8]

I'm not sure how far we can analyse the encounter of St John of the Cross as reflected here, in that the experience from which his words arise is of a particularly intimate union with God, and perhaps beyond analysis. Letting it rest as it is in our minds gives us an extreme picture, perhaps, as, comfortably or disturbingly, his image of the fiery probe and the torn robe are themselves indicative of an invasive and indefinable union, which breathes energy and a vital engagement.

The 'sweet encounter' cannot be denied, nor can the writer of the Song of Songs reach a conclusion that is at variance from this exposure and insight. The picture, created by our midday reading, builds from one metaphor to another. The winter is over, the rain is gone, the flowers are appearing, and all the signs of new life are apparent in the birds, fruit and blossom. The selection of verses from the Song of Songs, that we are considering at this moment, may lack the flame and the fiery probe, but are acutely sharpening the force of the stanza of St John of the Cross, which itself speaks of the tender force of the attention of God to the loving soul.

In the quiet of our afternoon walk or nap, we may like to dwell on the gentle consequences of these thoughts. Let me return to Evelyn Underhill's quotation from the beginning of today. She reminds us of the splendour and the truth that remain eternally, not to be affected

---

[8] *Poems of St John of the Cross*, Roy Campbell (Harvill, 1951), p. 29.

in any way by our desires and longings. This is saying something in a less poetic way than the two other authors just quoted. No fiery probes or tender doe-like glances through a lattice, but Christ before us in an everlasting presence reaching out, and that presence coming with concern for our welfare and need. The moment of opening is also the moment of unburdening, and so the words of Christ will be particularly important in grounding this reflection where *the truth that brings meaning to the world*, calls us to place our thoughts and prayers. This is a time for a few verses from the Gospels. Can I suggest you choose a short passage and use it as a dwelling place for the afternoon.

PRAYER

Christ,
O living flame of love,
let the glance of your eyes
pierce the lattice of my heart,
and warm the cold places of my being
with your merciful presence,
this day and always
Amen.

DAY 2
Evening

Song of Songs 2:13b-15

> *Arise, my love, my fair one,*
> *and come away.*
> *O my dove, in the clefts of the rock,*
> *in the covert of the cliff,*
> *let me see your face,*
> *let me hear your voice;*
> *for your voice is sweet,*
> *and your face is lovely.*
> *Catch us the foxes,*
> *the little foxes,*
> *that ruin the vineyards –*
> *for our vineyards are in blossom.*

THE EVENING IS a time when for most people work or school is over and the moment of relaxation takes over. There are those who can never part from the demands that family life, health or work places upon them, but for very many the shedding of responsibility for a few hours as the evening falls is a common enough experience. There is the possibility of the closing of the front door and preparing a meal, sitting in a comfortable corner or opening ourselves to a hobby or book or television programme or game with accompanying

Moments of Love

chat, drink, and a potter in the garden or whatever may be our way of relaxing. As we think of these things, we take up our early evening reflection and consider the element of hiding away, amongst all of those things that could potentially occupy the last daylight hours as dusk falls.

The cleft in the rock and covert of the cliff may put us in mind of the hymn, 'Rock of Ages cleft for me', if we are of the tradition, age and era of its familiarity. In the case of this hymn, the image of the crack in the rock is a hiding place that can only be Christ. The Song of Songs is also managing a picture of safety in God, as we find also in some of the psalms, but this is as much to do with the encounter as the hiding, and it could be said that the hymn follows this thought too. The emphasis on the comforting binding together of two people in a place of security is one that often complements the individual's experience of walking with another. Walking and talking together with someone we love is a common enough experience, and the time spent is enriched with hearing another's voice and seeing another's face. The adjectives sweet and lovely are not out of place either, as two loving people exclude the world within their personal cleft or covert. The image is delicately balanced between a safe sanctuary and an intimate encounter.

The introduction of the foxes in the text is an interesting and somewhat jarring change of idea, as sanctuary and intimacy become a riot of activity amidst the order of a vineyard in blossom. This disruption is temporary, as we shall return to the cleft in the rock before night falls today. Spiritually, for many of us, there are frequent moments when the discipline arranged

Day 2

about our lives of work and personal life unravels, and the young foxes at play in the vineyard are an apt description of the sense of chaos that we feel descends at that instant. It takes different forms, too. The intimacy of the encounter could throw up disturbing challenges, but equally such happiness of mood that for either reason, the simple pattern of disciplined devotion becomes disrupted, temporally at least.

The end of a second day of retreat finds us settled, or not, as the case may be, but to know that this potential ruffling of our peace of mind is normal is a help. So, let the young foxes run and play in the neat rows of vines and focus on the blossom which augurs well for a fruitful harvest, rather than the activity that may stir the few hours unrestfully, but will not seriously disrupt the retreat.

PRAYER

O Lord, as evening falls.
bless me, and all whom I love, as I rest in you.
Grant within the sanctuary of my heart
the grace of your healing presence,
that any disturbance of mind or spirit
may lead to acts of kindness,
and a strengthening of my faith,
a desire for firmer commitment,
and an increased resilience
to the trials and temptations of
this fleeting world, through the strength
and inspiration of your Holy Spirit.
Amen.

DAY 2
Night

Song of Songs 2:16-17

> *My beloved is mine and I am his;*
> *he pastures his flock among the lilies.*
> *Until the day breathes*
> *and the shadows flee,*
> *turn, my beloved, be like a gazelle*
> *or a young stag on the cleft mountains.*

IT IS STRANGE to be thinking of shadows fleeing at the close of the day, but, of course, they do; as the darkness falls there is no bright light to form the shadows of which the author speaks. The day breathes and the shadows lengthen then flee as we prepare for sleep, and step out from the cleft, lightly, like a gazelle or young stag. The air is still, the night is young, the cleft is to our side, the day's encounter is behind us, and we remain still and at peace.

The flock is pastured in the meadows below us, in the valley with the lilies. The foxes have gone, the world is turning to bring light and new day somewhere, as the sun lights up their sky, but for us, for now, it is the hour of darkness and the time of restoration and sleep. This is the hour that Nicodemus approached Jesus with a compulsion;

Day 2

he was attracted, but he had questions too, and a readiness to learn. That sense of possession that we find at the beginning of tonight's reading could be said to be present as Jesus talked with Nicodemus that night and spoke of the new birth that Christ instils in those who turn to him in faith and love. It is a subject to which we shall return, but enough for one day. Let us lie down and take our rest, for the Lord is watching over us and granting us sleep.

PRAYER

Father,
as shadows flee, and the day breathes
its dying breeze of its closing hours,
grant me a restful night,
deep and refreshing sleep,
and a heart at rest in you,
in the fellowship of the Holy Spirit,
within the love of Christ Jesus.
Amen.

DAY 3
The Quest

DAY 3
Morning

Song of Songs 3:1-2

> *Upon my bed at night*
> *I sought him whom my soul loves;*
> *I sought him, but found him not;*
> *I called him, but he gave no answer.*
> *'I will rise now and go about the city,*
> *in the streets and in the squares;*
> *I will seek him whom my soul loves.'*
> *I sought him, but found him not.*

WE BEGIN DAY 3 with a dream. A dream is all very well, but can a search for love, growing out of that dream, as one eases into full consciousness from sleep, be experienced in a way that leads to the revelation of God's love for us? Is the search such that we can wake out of sleep with a greater determination than ever to find the object of our search? The source of the allegory is not difficult for us to imagine. Someone wakes from sleep with a delightful thought in their head: 'Today I am going to find the one I love.' Once ready for the day, with this thought playing in the mind, with clarity and determination, this crystallises into, 'I will look and enquire, and walk, and go

Moments of Love

where I expect to find, searching all the time.'

Translating this from the allegory to reality, the words of Jesus are echoed here, as he who insisted that that searching is never an unfulfilled quest:

> *'Ask, and it will be given to you; search, and you will find; knock, and the door will be opened for you. For everyone who asks receives, and everyone who searches finds, and for everyone who knocks, the door will be opened.'* (Matthew 7:7-8)

But in this Song of Songs, it is beginning with a dream. Now, avoiding the fancifulness that can slip so easily into these thoughts, let us consider with care and attention what waking from the dream that has stimulated us to action, is going to promote, by way of spiritual enrichment. The dream is to be understood to have been no ordinary dream, and the sleep from which it arose no normal night of rest. St John of the Cross expands his verse on this sleep with his explanation regarding, 'the tranquil night'. First, let us expand stanza XV from which this description arises:

> *The tranquil night*
> *At the approaches of the dawn,*
> *The silent music,*
> *The murmuring solitude,*
> *The supper which revives, and enkindles love.*

The English translation by David Lewis of both the verse and its commentary by St John of the Cross are in the idiom of the early-twentieth century, but the point is still quite clear:

Day 3

In this spiritual sleep in the bosom of the Beloved the soul is in possession and fruition of all the calm, repose and quiet of a peaceful night, and receives at the same time in God a certain dim, unfathomable divine intelligence.[9]

Kieran Kavanaugh's translation for the works of St John of the Cross in the *Classics of Western Spirituality* series published in 1987 chooses 'The Tranquil night', for his opening rendering of stanza XV, but then proceeds, beautifully translated, as follows:

At the time of the rising of the dawn,
Silent music,
Sounding solitude,
The supper that refreshes, and deepens love.[10]

As we begin a new day, arising in search of divine inspiration and full of desire for Christ's words and direction, the tranquil night of St John of the Cross is a point worth pondering. If this were possible to self-generate we would, no doubt, do it, but as we cannot control our dreams, neither can we, *receive(s) at the same time in God a certain dim, unfathomable divine intelligence.* We are in the realm of grace, beyond our strength and needing a spirit of a responsive, searching heart alone.

In the *Spiritual Canticle of the Soul* as in the Song of Songs itself, metaphors are mixed

---

[9] *A Spiritual Canticle of the Soul* (stanza on p. 10, commentary on p. 121).
[10] *John of the Cross: Selected Writings* (Paulist Press, 1987), p. 245.

and sections can be linked. In St John of the Cross's own explanation of the text, he does link this stanza with the previous one, and Keiran Kavanaugh follows the same pattern, which introduces the thought of the whisper of God coming in the tranquil night. Kavanaugh, translates this as the 'whistle of God', while David Lewis prefers, 'whisper'. However we may think of easing into consciousness from the dream of the tranquil night, the presence of a light breeze carrying the breath of God, whether thought of as a whisper or a low whistle, takes us back to Elijah on Mount Sinai and to other occasions in the scriptures when the voice of God is coming softly to the ear of one of his servants.

These are layers of interpretation being placed upon the dream, or at least semi-conscious imaginings of the author of the Song of Songs, but they ring true with the mind searching and calling with no answer in these first two verses of chapter 3. That light indication of the presence of the loved one in a whisper inside one's head, reflects the mind searching, and needing to go further, seek more diligently; putting other ideas to one side, the single-minded desire for the object of one's love is all-consuming. *Silent music, sounding solitude,* can describe the state of emptiness needing filling, *enkindling love*, and providing the impetus for the diligent search.

Day 3

PRAYER

Christ,
open my ears to your voice,
and my heart to your words.
Let this day reveal something more
to me, whose dull mind and frail life
cannot contain what I seek to know,
yet long to experience in fellowship
with my sisters and brothers in you,
now and to eternity.
Amen.

DAY 3
Midday

Song of Songs 3:3-5

> *The sentinels found me,*
> *as they went about in the city.*
> *'Have you seen him whom my soul loves?'*
> *Scarcely had I passed them,*
> *when I found him whom my soul loves.*
> *I held him, and would not let him go*
> *until I brought him into my mother's house,*
> *and into the chamber of her that conceived me.*
> *I adjure you, O daughters of Jerusalem,*
> *by the gazelles or the wild does:*
> *do not stir up or awaken love*
> *until it is ready!*

THIS MORNING THE search for the loved one from the moment of awakening from a dream, was translated into a listening for a whisper of God in the midst of the streets and squares of the city. The searcher now becomes the one who is found. How often it is that the experience of one who seeks to gain something or someone they desire, that the very opposite happens: the finding occurs when they are discovered, and the revelation is seen to be in the hands of the one

Day 3

who was sought. This is how we understand the finding of God. We may desire and search and then discover that Christ has been calling us all of the time, and we have been deaf to the whisper or, 'whistle' of God.

Well, the author of the Song of Songs has been found by sentinels and, so, understands the principle of our calling being initiated by Christ. He calls us to himself, but we may discover this when we are on the lookout ourselves. This idea is beautifully described in these verses, as scarcely have the sentinels been passed than the lovers meet, and find their way to a place of comfort and security. There is a rounded sense of completion in this flow of dream leading to longing and searching, to being found, united and brought to a place of safety and love, that rings true of our daily call to devotion to Christ. We may not rest there long, but as we come to our quiet time or daily office or whatever is our practice of prayer, from some such opening as, *'Lord, open my lips; and our mouth shall proclaim your praise'*, to our closing petition, whatever it may be. It is the routine and repetitive nature of this practice that marks our day as committed to Christ, who calls us to himself, and to discipleship in his name; a daily recapturing of the call and response, as reflected in these verses.

Is this the 'awakening of love' of which the author proceeds to develop the train of thought? My feeling is that it is. If we are brought to the place of comfort and safety in prayer, in fellowship with Christ, we are also being united in a love that expresses itself in a fresh breath of life. The Song of Songs expresses a sense of life and love – and indeed beauty and joy – with

Moments of Love

the grace of a gazelle or a wild doe. Maybe not on the mountainside here, but the implication of sensitivity and energy and youth is, nonetheless, within these verses. There is a sense that one thought upon another is leading us this day, from the opening dream through the encounter after the search, to the place of not only security, but inspired intention and renewed life and hope.

This speaks to us of opportunity and a further adventure in faith on day three of our retreat. Are we ready for such a thing? When we read these verses at age 20, or 40 or 65 or 90, can we feel the same passion and hope? Yes, of course we can. Christ is the same yesterday, today and forever, and in his sight and within his fellowship we are as a gazelle and wild doe, with love stirred by his presence and place within us. This is the day of hope, no matter what. Rejoice and be glad in it.

PRAYER

Heavenly Father,
at this midday hour, as I have thoughts
surrounding my place in your sight,
and in the calling of your Son, Jesus,
may I feel and know the new life that
the loving encounter brings to all
who are united in that love.
Prepare me for what lies ahead,
that I may, without fear, tread the path
along which you are calling me.
In Christ Jesus I pray.
Amen.

DAY 3
Evening

Song of Songs 3:6-8

> *What is that coming up from the wilderness,*
> *like a column of smoke,*
> *perfumed with myrrh and frankincense,*
> *with all the fragrant powders of the merchant?*
> *Look, it is the litter of Solomon!*
> *Around it are sixty mighty men*
> *of the mighty men of Israel,*
> *all equipped with swords*
> *and expert in war,*
> *each with his sword at his thigh*
> *because of alarms by night.*

THESE VERSES AND those that follow tonight are recording a scene of the procession of a bridegroom's retinue towards his wedding, and seen to be Solomon's. So, there is grandeur and expensive accoutrements and fragrances, and the secure band of soldiers, bring all to see that there is someone important coming and something important about to happen. This chapter of the Song of Songs that began with a searching in the streets of the city for the one who is loved, ends the quest with the journey to the place of the wedding. In so far as we can interpret this with a message for us today, it surely lies in the seeking and being found, as we recalled earlier.

Solomon, for all his wisdom, and perhaps as a result of it, was a powerful king and judge of his people, and successfully pushed back the boundaries of his nation state, expanding the area of his influence and wealth. The notion that a faithful servant of God is rewarded with wealth and success is one that we continue to encounter today, both individually and in parishes and other religious communities as well. But is the quest for wealth and success compatible with the quest about which we have been thinking today? That may be putting it too directly, as churches that are wealthy and numerically strong would not necessarily claim that that is what they have sought to be. Rather, it has just happened because they are faithful and are blessed in carrying the message of Christ to the world and many have been brought to salvation within the holy and blessed family of the Church. The wealth that has accrued has allowed the work of ministry and discipling the membership to continue and expand. In other words this is not wealth, as such, it is fundamentally resources for mission. Still, the question remains ever relevant, 'If wealth has increased, have you set your heart upon it?' As we know, the more one has, the more one wants.

Seeing Solomon in all his glory, stirring up the dust of the wilderness into a cloud like smoke such are the numbers attending him, is a fitting picture as a backdrop to this quest, or question, as the evening falls and we prepare for a quiet few hours before bed. I rather think that the dust

Day 3

cloud would be inclined to hide the fragrance and the powders of the merchants, but perhaps when one is in the midst of the activity the dust is less thick and the scents more stimulating. Whatever is reason for it, perhaps wishful thinking in the heat and activity of the train, the words of chapter 3 are recording something of beauty in the midst of a desert procession. Maybe a timely reminder that not all quests are without ulterior motives, some disconnected enjoyment or self-satisfaction being a supplement to the search or calling that we are undertaking. This, as we know, is a danger for churches as much as for individuals.

PRAYER

Jesus Christ,
the same yesterday, today and forever,
the Way, the Truth and the Life,
restore in me a quest for the pure beauty of holiness,
that I know is in undimmed fellowship in you,
day by day and hour by hour.
Keep me from the temptation to seek my own glory,
worldly success and comfort, and keep my eyes on you,
in whom and through whom I pray.
Amen.

DAY 3
Night

Song of Songs 3:9-11

> *King Solomon made himself a palanquin*
> *from the wood of Lebanon.*
> *He made its posts of silver,*
> *its back of gold, its seat of purple;*
> *its interior was inlaid with love.*
> *Daughters of Jerusalem,*
> *come out.*
> *Look, O daughters of Zion,*
> *at King Solomon,*
> *at the crown with which his mother crowned him*
> *on the day of his wedding,*
> *on the day of the gladness of his heart.*

EARLIER THIS EVENING we had a session that reminded us of the singleminded-ness of heart of the follower of Christ. Having taken that thought to its conclusion in refining our sight of things of beauty and abundance and extravagance, let us not fear to enjoy them. Wealth only presents a problem when it becomes the object of the quest, even in a hidden secondary way underneath more noble aspirations for the Christian. We close this day, then, rejoicing in the array of King Solomon on the day of his wedding, his palanquin made of

Day 3

the most precious of worked timber, silver and gold – and all 'inlaid in love.' The creation of objects of beauty with love is a supplementary quest that has long and honourable tradition. Our churches are adorned in this way, as expressions of worship of the deepest love and desire for thanksgiving and offering, knowing that what is given is rewarded and renewed over and over again, as worshippers in the future take pleasure, and have their hearts lifted by what is before them.

Motive is the element of the quest that we have been thinking about for half of today, and it is a worthy reflection for part of our retreat. Before we pass on tomorrow to other things and later consider our attitude to those less physically or mentally able, or possessing less than we have of this world's goods, let us leave this purely where it affects us and our search for the truth that is in Christ, without hypocrisy or rejection of the very real blessings of things of earthly value, beauty or the art work of human hands and imagination. Whether lovely words, or music, or visual art, dance, gorgeous attire, or objects of rare and unimaginable refinement, fragrance and texture, may these things lift our hearts and minds to God, rather than to acquisition and possession. Solomon received a crown, committed himself in marriage and received gladness of heart, and all was witnessed and celebrated within the calling to be King of Israel with all its responsibilities, and that was his context, whilst ours have our relationships, sources of happiness crowned in a myriad of different ways, but none less important than that of this great monarch, who just happened to be who he was, whilst you are you, and I am me. Thank the Lord!

Moments of Love

PRAYER

Father,
at the end of this day of searching
from city streets for one loved,
to the source of happiness and motivation
for my life, in all its beauty and desires,
keep me this night, and always, conscious
 of who I am,
happy in the knowledge that that is what you
 want of me,
in the company of those I love, and in
 fellowship
with your Son, Jesus Christ.
Amen.

DAY 4
Beauty

DAY 4
Morning

Song of Songs 4:1-4

> *How beautiful you are, my love,*
> *how very beautiful!*
> *Your eyes are doves*
> *behind your veil.*
> *Your hair is like a flock of goats,*
> *moving down the slopes of Gilead.*
> *Your teeth are like a flock of shorn ewes*
> *that have come up from the washing,*
> *all of which bear twins,*
> *and not one among them is bereaved.*
> *Your lips are like a crimson thread,*
> *and your mouth is lovely.*
> *Your cheeks are like halves of a pomegranate*
> *behind your veil.*
> *Your neck is like the tower of David,*
> *built in courses;*
> *on it hang a thousand bucklers,*
> *all of them shields of warriors.*

WE LEFT THE bridegroom last night in a state of gorgeous array for the wedding, as comfort and joy are expressed in opulent celebration and extravagance. Now the bridegroom looks upon the

Moments of Love

bride and much of today's readings extol her beauty.

My wife and I walk most days around our village and the lanes and country paths over the hills and through the glens that surround us. We are blessed with living in a very lovely and steep sided valley, and our village is full of trees and has the high rainfall and westerly aspect to have elements of temperate rainforest within it too, with dripping moss and lichen, a meeting of two rivers bringing water off the hills, creating fine waterfalls both within the village and not far beyond it. As we walk, my wife says that she is inclined to see the small things at our feet, whilst I more often look up, at the birds and the trees and the sky. Like most generalisations it is not always true, but between us we prompt each other to look at what one or other of us may otherwise miss. I'm sure that we are like other couples or groups of friends, bringing things of beauty or interest to each other's notice. Writing down what we see is another matter. Recording observations is a process requiring dedication and a desire not to forget. Hence the diary, the memoir, and the autobiography.

The bridegroom is recording the entrancement of his eyes, as he looks upon his bride. We will continue his musings later, but even this morning starts with her eyes, hair, teeth, lips, cheeks and neck. Eyes, like doves behind the veil, remind me of a Jane Austen novel, for Darcy was first entranced by Elizabeth in *Pride and Prejudice*, when enduring Miss Bingley's teasing: 'I have been meditating on the very great pleasure which a pair of fine eyes in the face of a pretty woman can bestow.'[11] With the bride veiled the

11   *Pride and Prejudice*, chapter 6.

Day 4

bridegroom cannot see the fine sparkling of her eyes, but they shine as doves through the thin fabric.

Gradually one simile upon another is built up as the bridegroom considers the physical beauty of the woman he loves, and to whom he is united. There is no need to make a direct parallel with these verses and the spiritual sense in which we read this Song of Songs, but it is enough for us to ponder on what we imagine is the *beauty* that we behold as we consider the captivating meaning of our desire for rapt attention to the encounter with Christ that brings us fulfilment. In Psalm 29 we read these words: 'Give unto the Lord the glory due unto his name; worship the Lord in the beauty of holiness' (verse 2), and find something similar in Psalm 96:8-9. The hymn, *O worship the Lord in the beauty of holiness* by John Samuel Bewley Monsell uses the precise words of Psalm 96 verse 9 in the Authorised Version for the hymn's opening line. However, Monsell relates his inspiration to 1 Chronicles 16: 29, placing this verse as a heading to his manuscript.[12] That verse runs:

> *Ascribe to the Lord the glory due his name;*
> *bring an offering, and come before him.*
> *Worship the Lord in holy splendour.*

In both of the psalms mentioned and in the text from 1 Chronicles chapter 16, the reference to beauty is subjective, and it is linked directly to holiness. In the Song of Songs chapter 4, which

---

[12] I am indebted for this observation to the *Companion to Church Hymnal* by Edward Darling and Donald Davison (Columba Press, 2005), p. 295.

we are pondering today, the beauty is indeed in the eye of the beholder, namely the bridegroom, but it is nevertheless a beauty seen with the eyes of love, rather than a beauty generated within the heart and viewed with the inner eye of faith. It is also connected to an offering in the 1 Chronicles reading, which is not insignificant.

Holiness, offering, beauty beheld, and before us we have a text from the Song of Songs that is romantically placing the tender glances of the lover on the one he loves, with references to the perception of the created world, to doves, goats, ewes, to a crimson thread, a pomegranate and the strength of a built tower adorned with the shields of the protectors. There appears to be no direct link between these similes and the thread of beauty, other than the step-by-step reference of each beautiful part of the bride's appearance finding context in fruitfulness, life and security. As we pull these disparate pictures together, let us try and inject the themes of holiness and offering with the over-riding principle that God is worshipped in beauty. Not in the beauty of the physical eye, such as is the bridegroom's, but in the inner sanctuary of the heart's desire for holiness and self-offering.

In this capacity for what is beautiful for Christ, we should recall his anointing at Bethany, and look at that context. In Matthew 26:10, and in the equivalent text in Mark, we read of his anointing by the woman with the alabaster jar as being a 'beautiful act'. It is the only occasion upon which Jesus makes such an observation of beauty, but the word *kalos* (fair, beautiful) in the Greek text can be adapted according to its object, and in the case of its association with *ergon* (work,

Day 4

task, action) it can be rendered as 'good' rather than 'beautiful'. The NRSV made this change from the original RSV, where *kalos* is given as beautiful.

It seems to me that we can claim from this mix of references to beauty and divine human relationships that however we may confuse matters subjectively and objectively, beauty in essence is of the soul, if I may use that word to denote in some sense the ground of our being. So, we are emotionally and spiritually affected by beauty. The author of the Song of Songs is rhapsodising poetically by containing this thought within the physical attraction of a man and a woman, but the extension, as I understand it through the psalms (and the hymns based upon them), is that this is also including, essentially, a desire to give and a longing for holiness, in their purest and highest aspirations before God. We shall return to this thought later.

PRAYER

Almighty and gracious God and Father,
in the beauty of holiness,
and in the love of your creation,
I offer myself and all I have to you.
Grant me purity of heart and eyes
to see the actions of beauty, mercy and love
in the day-to-day encounters of my life,
in Christ Jesus my Lord.
Amen.

DAY 4
Midday

Song of Songs 4:5-8

> *Your two breasts are like two fawns,*
> *twins of a gazelle,*
> *that feed among the lilies.*
> *Until the day breathes*
> *and the shadows flee,*
> *I will hasten to the mountain of myrrh*
> *and the hill of frankincense.*
> *You are altogether beautiful, my love;*
> *there is no flaw in you.*
> *Come with me from Lebanon, my bride;*
> *come with me from Lebanon.*
> *Depart from the peak of Amana,*
> *from the peak of Senir and Hermon,*
> *from the dens of lions,*
> *from the mountains of leopards.*

THE MIDDLE OF the day, and we are touching a more intimate expression of the bridegroom's attention than earlier. His contemplation of the bride's physical attraction brings him to liken her breasts to beautiful things, and his blissful thoughts take him to the beauty of the hills and the mountains, an area that we now know of as

Day 4

the Golan Heights. There are peaks covered in winter snow and the lower slopes where fruit trees thrive in the cool but sunny climate. At one time lions and leopards would have been a danger to travellers in the region. The writer is embracing more than one thought in these verses, as we find in other parts of this intriguing book. The likening of youthfulness and beauty to the gazelle on the hills is one that we have experienced already, but in other ways this is a further development of the verses that we considered earlier today.

Fragrance is a thread that runs through the whole work and brings another of our senses into play, which is surely what the author intends. The eyes lead the imagination from the woman's breasts to the heights of Hermon, but the analogy is understood as part of the allegory too. In stanza xxxvi of his *Spiritual Canticle of the Soul* St John of the Cross comments on this going forth and considering beauty and the hills and mountains, yet containing beauty within ourselves. Kieran Kavanaugh's translation of the Spanish runs:

> *Let us rejoice, beloved,*
> *And let us go forth to behold ourselves in your*
>   *beauty,*
> *To the mountain and to the hill,*
> *To where the pure water flows,*
> *And further deep into the thicket.*[13]

The key element of this is the line: *let us go forth to behold ourselves in your beauty.* St John of the Cross adds the comment: 'This means: Let us so act that by means of this loving activity we may attain to the

---

[13] Ibid., p. 274.

vision of ourselves in your beauty in eternal life. That is: That I may be so transformed in your beauty that we may be alike in beauty, and both behold ourselves in your beauty, possessing now your very beauty ...'
The passage continues in this vein for some lines further.

It is a problematic issue with the Song of Songs that the sheer variety and repetition of similes and metaphors, entwined with a strong allegorical underlying theme, make for confusion. But if we can tease out the place of beauty in this day it will help, and St John of the Cross assists us, for what he is saying is that loving activity, in itself, is something beautiful. Chapter 4 began with beauty in the eyes of the bridegroom looking upon the bride, but the unfolding pictures that develop throughout the chapter demonstrate that the beauty of the woman is related to the overwhelmingly beautiful aura of creation.

What I read from this is that the subjective experience that we may describe in terms of 'beauty is in the eye of the beholder', is in fact even deeper and more profound than even that helpful reckoning. There is feeling and spiritual nourishment in understanding that we have been touched in a way that has generated a sense of beauty within us. It happens, for example, as wild swimmers or practitioners of other extreme sports, find a release of endorphins and other hormones in the brain; so beauty can assail us with a rush of emotion and a surge of spiritual wellbeing. We may be enraptured by a work of art, or entranced by a piece of music; so the bridegroom's sight of the beauty of his bride is stirring a deeper sense of wellbeing and beauty and spiritual fulfilment.

This has been quite an intense period of

Day 4

thought today, and to rest in something beautiful for ourselves is an aim for this afternoon. Perhaps a walk, if the weather is clement or a comfortable sit and read, with a not-too-heavy book, or maybe just a sleep!

PRAYER

Heavenly Father,
in the moment of beautiful thoughts
bring me a sense that such beauty
lies at the heart of creation both physical and
    spiritual.
Let me rest today in the peace of your
    presence,
and order my life in accord with your will,
in Jesus Christ my Lord.
Amen.

DAY 4
Evening

Song of Songs 4:9-15

*You have ravished my heart, my sister, my bride,
you have ravished my heart with a glance of your eyes,
with one jewel of your necklace.
How sweet is your love, my sister, my bride!
how much better is your love than wine,
and the fragrance of your oils than any spice!
Your lips distil nectar, my bride;
honey and milk are under your tongue;
the scent of your garments is like the scent of Lebanon.
A garden locked is my sister, my bride,
a garden locked, a fountain sealed.
Your channel is an orchard of pomegranates
with all choicest fruits,
henna with nard,
nard and saffron, calamus and cinnamon,
with all trees of frankincense,
myrrh and aloes,
with all chief spices—
a garden fountain, a well of living water,
and flowing streams from Lebanon.*

Day 4

WITH MORE ACCOLADES as to the beauty of the bride we begin our evening reflection. We are still in the mountains bordering Lebanon; the gardens of their hearts are locked against other lovers, as the pull of other gods and temptations to apostasy are excluded. Anyone who has been to this area of the country will be aware of the remains of the shrine to the Greek god Pan at Banias (Caesarea Philippi in the New Testament) near a natural spring forming the Banias River, one of the sources of the River Jordan, but more ancient are the references to the Syrian goddess of the mountains, both in this area and in northern Syria. So, the beautiful garden locked and the flowing pure mountain water held safe for the untainted encounter of love is understandable. The water runs from the spring in channels, clear and cold out of the face of the rock and the author of the Song of Songs is making much of the fruits that grow from the well-watered ground, maybe not pomegranates there, but perhaps in the valleys that the water will reach. Henna and saffron are dyes, calamus is a herb of boggy ground with a sweet taste, and, like rushes, may have been used to scent the floors of houses, whilst cinnamon, frankincense, myrrh are spices, and aloes is a succulent with healing properties.

The richness of the fruits of the land springing from the abundance of water from the mountains is the emphasis of these verses; *a garden fountain, a well of living water, and flowing streams from Lebanon.* This is not difficult to translate into a refreshment of the soul, as beauty in the eyes becomes a perceived beauty within the heart, in the encounter with Christ bridegroom of the bride of the Church and expressed in Eucharistic fellowship and divine love.

PRAYER

O Lord,
the source of living water,
from the well at Sychar to the font of baptism,
from the flowing channels of the mountain
    streams
to the flood waters that bring life to the
    desert.
Refresh my soul with your presence,
and wash me within,
today and always.
Amen.

DAY 4
Evening

Song of Songs 4:16

> *O north wind,*
> *and come, O south wind!*
> *Blow upon my garden*
> *that its fragrance may be wafted abroad.*
> *Let my beloved come to his garden,*
> *and eat its choicest fruits.*

IN THE EVENING there comes a welcome breeze, from north or from south, it matters not at all. It is where it is blowing that is noted here. It is blowing upon the garden of the loving heart. There is no difficulty in us translating this into thoughts of the breath of the Holy Spirit. The imagery is of the New Testament, as it is of the Old. We feel the wind, no matter where it comes from or to whither it goes, it is its breath upon us that matters and this wind wafts a fragrance with it.

So, we end this fourth day in the garden with the breath of God whispering a freshness after the day in which we may feel sated with beauty, so much have we contemplated the effect of the allure of human attraction, and that of flower, fruit and the works of our hands in treasured wood and precious metals. Avoiding the possessiveness to which these things so often lead is our night-time freedom from this particular burden. We do this in the waft of the evening breeze, and settle ourselves to a restful sleep in the mood of confidence in commending our souls to the protection of God for the coming night.

I will lay me down and take my sleep, surrounded by the angels. Like a child resting without a care in the world, I shall approach the hours of darkness in complete peace of mind, having prayed my concerns away, leaving them with Christ in total trust that all will be well.

PRAYER

Lord,
I lie down in peace,
with your Spirit wafting a divine breath
upon my weary soul.
I pray for a restful night
that I may see afresh
feel renewed, ready for your will
to be revealed to me
tomorrow, at dawn and through the day,
your gift through whatever life may bring.
Amen.

DAY 5
The Wound of Love

DAY 5
Morning

Song of Songs 5:1

> *I come to my garden, my sister, my bride;*
> *I gather my myrrh with my spice,*
> *I eat my honeycomb with my honey,*
> *I drink my wine with my milk.*
>
> *Eat, friends, drink,*
> *and be drunk with love.*

TODAY BEGINS WHERE yesterday ended, in the garden. Not now with the evening breeze denoting the presence of the Holy Spirit, whither it comes and whither it goes, unknown, but the place of feeling is all the experience that is needed. This morning, the gathering and eating and drinking are marking the new day in the company of one loved and loving in return. So, the day is launched for us in sweetness and with the spice and wine of luxury. It is comfortable and restful and all is ease and happiness.

I come to my garden, my sister, my bride. The fifth day of the retreat is beginning in the place of peace and contentment. This is surely part of any retreat that extends for more than 36-48 hours, that we grant ourselves an escape from thought and directed prayer? Where, I wonder, is the garden of your delight? It may not be a garden at all, but some special place of safety, inspiration, joy and fulfilment. A place from which you exclude all the pressing realities of daily life and concern. A place of sanctuary and restoration. A place from which one moves forward to try new things, resume old battles, face fresh challenges, remind oneself of commitments that intrude daily, if not hourly, upon one's conscience. But, for now, for this morning, for this day, lay them aside and allow yourself to escape. Inhabit the space of the child, visit the secret garden, feel the soil of growing things, smell the spice, herb and sweetness of vegetation, gather the blossoms of the fruiting shrubs, follow the bees to their flowers and the cattle to their pasture, hold the ripe grains and berries of autumn with the first lovely blooms of spring, with a warm summer sun on your face and the soft snow of winter quietly falling in the silent still world that is yours today. *Eat, friends, drink, and be drunk with love.*

You are not alone in this garden of your delight, for you have come to this place, because Christ is with you. Let us imagine within this garden there is a pond, reflecting the stillness of the whole place, and on it, in the silence of this moment look upon it. Fr Andrew (aka Henry Ernest Hardy) an Anglican priest and contemplative of a century ago wrote the following poem of an encounter between God and Man:

The Pool
I pray my soul may be a pool,
A pool of silent love;
I pray that on the face of it

Day 5

The Holy Ghost may move;
I pray that he may make it pure
With his own purity,
Still, but not stagnant,
Fresh and clear with His own liberty,
Unfathomed as the ocean deep
Of God's own charity;
So may its waters cleanse and heal
And comfort weary feet,
May every bitterness be gone
And may their taste be sweet.
May Christ my Master drink of it;
As once by Jacob's well
A poor smirched woman saw Him sit
And heard Him tidings tell
Of living water He would give,
How, drinking it, Her soul should live
And yet He asked of her
That she should give Him to drink
Love's cup of water there,
So I will even dare to think
That I might follow her.
But this beyond all else I pray,
That, mirrored, He may see
On some divine and distant day
In His own time, in His own way,
Himself look out from me.[14]

The closing words of this poem, which becomes a prayer, lift our indulgent morning of peaceful restoration to the hope of where, 'Love's cup of water' may take us. The metaphor is subtly changed from water that refreshes and renews,

---

[14] *Love's Fulfilment: An Anthology from the Writings of Father Andrew* (Mowbray, 1957), pp. 105-6.

to water that reflects in its stillness as a pool. This prayer is not calling for action; not calling for us to change direction from the desire to rest in the garden this morning. It is merely an acknowledgement that by so resting in the place of beauty with Christ that something of his nature be imprinted upon us that may change our face to the world.

PRAYER

Lord Jesus,
walk with me, as through a garden
full of the beauty of your creation,
may the pace be slow,
and my eyes be sensitive to everything
around and through which we pass.
Glance upon me Lord, and,
through the eyes of faith,
bless me with a look of love for those
I shall walk with in the coming days.
In some divine and distant day,
in your own time and in your own day,
I pray that you may look out from me.
Amen.

DAY 5
Midday

Song of Songs 5:2-6

*I slept, but my heart was awake.
Listen! my beloved is knocking.
'Open to me, my sister, my love,
my dove, my perfect one;
for my head is wet with dew,
my locks with the drops of the night.'
I had put off my garment;
how could I put it on again?
I had bathed my feet;
how could I soil them?
My beloved thrust his hand into the opening,
and my inmost being yearned for him.
I arose to open to my beloved,
and my hands dripped with myrrh,
my fingers with liquid myrrh,
upon the handles of the bolt.
I opened to my beloved,
but my beloved had turned and was gone.
My soul failed me when he spoke.
I sought him, but did not find him;
I called him, but he gave no answer.*

Moments of Love

WE BEGAN DAY 3 with a dream. Day 5 has another. Sleep holds the lover in anticipation, as one wet with dew on the threshold of the place of desire. The elements of patient hope are present: the end of the night of waiting, the gentle fall of the dampness of early morning dripping from the ends of her hair, reflecting the refreshing grace-filled longing that is to be fulfilled. Closeness and purity of thought and intention are spoken through the 'my sister, my love, my dove' as the perfection of the moment appears as the dream holds a wakened heart as well as a resting body.

There is something more happening here. There is something in the encounter that builds upon the desire to mirror the look of Christ upon another, and receive the glance upon us too in the meeting. Let us look at the elements that the author is weaving into this dreamy dialogue. Shedding a garment suggests putting off a mask or outer display of carefully arranged virtue; feet-washing is very easily linked with Christ for the Christian to both offer and receive; putting one's hand into an opening is a gesture of vulnerability. The origins of the expression 'Chance your Arm' of history or myth[15] relates to the ending of

---

[15] In 1492, two Irish families, the Butlers of Ormonde and the FitzGeralds of Kildare, were involved in a serious dispute, with violent fighting between the two families. The violence spiralled out of control, and the Butlers retreated to the Chapter House of Saint Patrick's Cathedral, Dublin. The FitzGeralds followed them and pleaded with them to come out and make peace, but, frightened of the potential trap, the Butlers refused.

Gerald FitzGerald took the initiative and ordered that a hole be cut in the door. He then put his arm

Day 5

one feud at the Chapter House of St Patrick's Cathedral in Dublin, as the arm of one combatant reached through a hacked hole in the outer door to grasp the hand of another in a gesture of peace. However this gesture may be imagined, we risk damage to ourselves by leaving ourselves in another's power. All of these examples of a yearning for restoration and loving encounter, show an openness to another that grows from that very walk in the garden this morning, standing at the pool of reflection, seeking the mirrored face of Christ. The dream is over. *'I arose to open to my beloved, and my hands dripped with myrrh, my fingers with liquid myrrh, upon the handles of the bolt.'*

The outcome of this openness in this text is not what we expect: *'I opened to my beloved, but my beloved had turned and was gone.'* What is this absence saying to us? The hard but important lesson is that though we are seekers and live in expectation of finding, of knocking and finding the door opening to our push, of expecting that we have only to ask and we shall receive, that we shall also know the time and place of God – we must remember that God's thoughts are not our thoughts, neither God's ways, ours. Encountering God in the stillness and silence of a retreat may mean withdrawal from the feeling presence to the knowing of faith; the experience of the darkness that speaks of the reality of the light; the emptiness that expresses the underlying need within us for filling with Christ's life. We are not

through the door, offering his hand to those on the other side. Seeing that FitzGerald was willing to risk his arm by putting it through the door, the Butlers recognised this for what it was, a serious gesture for peace. They shook hands through the hole.

generating the feelings of ecstasy ourselves; the desire for the encounter with the divine, is, after all, the Way of the Cross.

So, fear not, nor be downhearted, if the garden of our delight is not a spiritual paradise, but a lesson in knowing the wound of love that brings us a deeper knowledge and a step or two further in understanding the place that you have at the table in the Kingdom, where broken bread and shed wine are the sweet honey and the myrrh of our prayerful state, as we knock and open ourselves to the fire of love with which we shall be refined, and in whose consuming presence our experience of true love is perfected.

PRAYER

Christ Jesus,
be present with me through this day.
At this midday hour may I know
that my feelings and thoughts
are even now within your hand.
Show me what to truly desire,
as I reach out to touch and seek your love,
forgiveness and direction.
Keep my heart alive with hope,
my intention calm and reassured,
my life committed in faith,
which is beyond sound and sight
and held ever in your compassionate mercy.
Amen.

DAY 5
Evening

Song of Songs 5:7-8

> *Making their rounds in the city*
> *the sentinels found me;*
> *they beat me, they wounded me,*
> *they took away my mantle,*
> *those sentinels of the walls.*
> *I adjure you, O daughters of Jerusalem,*
> *if you find my beloved,*
> *tell him this:*
> *I am faint with love.*

THE DREAM OF chapter 5 has a different conclusion to the dream of chapter 3:1-5. The withdrawal of conscious awareness of the lover's presence is deepening into sorrow and pain at the beating, wounding and stripping of those whose help had been sought earlier. Christian theologians of the Medieval period such as Bernard of Clairvaux, writing on mystical union, emphasised that language was insufficient to describe the encounter, yet he and others are drawn to the Song of Songs by way of its metaphors. If Bernard's unfinished sermons of the *Song of Songs* in his best-known work *Sermones super Cantica Canticorum* are designed to promote the idea that God must be loved simply, and with ardent discipline, purely because he *is* God, then the pain of absence, and the wounds that are felt because of the unfulfilled desire emphasised by that absence, is something that we must embrace with care and attention.

Amy Hollywood writes in her essay *Mysticism and Transcendence*, '[Yet] following in the tradition inaugurated by Origen, Bernard insists on the spiritual nature of the senses whose experiences are elicited and described through biblical language.'[16] The rejection section of the dream in chapter 5 of the *Song of Songs* is no less real in its interpretation of the spiritual state than that of the walk in the garden at the beginning of the dream. Hollywood also identifies that in the thirteenth century the line between one experience and another, and the apprehension of the divine between the physical and the spiritual, was becoming less defined.

Being *faint with love* may be both a weakening of heart, soul and spirit because of unrequited love, and, at the same time, faintness through unfulfilled desire. However we may draw these moments of the dream into some kind of order, the conclusion suggests that love can wound as well as heal. This is not a surprise. If we were to lose the capacity to love we would lose compassion, sensitivity and the vulnerability that comes from opening ourselves to another, and offering them our life. One who loves is one who accepts the wounds that cannot be avoided. But, we would have it no other way, for love's

[16] The essay appears in *Christianity in Western Europe c.1100 – c.1500, Volume 4 of The Cambridge History of Christianity* (Cambridge, 2009), p. 304.

Day 5

risk is love's gift and love's strength as well.

But we are not left there, are we? As St John of the Cross emphasises in his poems, the wounds of love are only healed by the presence of love:

*For pains acquired so dearly
From love, cannot recover
Save only through the presence of the lover.*

*O brook of crystal sheen,
Could you but cause, upon your silver fine,
Suddenly to be seen
The eyes for which I pine
Which in my inmost heart my thoughts design!*

*Withhold their gaze, my Love,
For I take wing.*[17]

PRAYER

Father
I offer to you the love that I hold,
and by offering it release it.
It is a poor offering, but it is real
for with it I bare my soul's wounds.
In joy I step out afresh with love to share,
keeping my eyes on the scars on hands
and feet and side of your dear Son,
who died for love of my love,
Jesus Christ my Lord.
Amen.

---

[17] *Poems of St John of the Cross,* pp. 17-18.

DAY 5
Night

Song of Songs 5:9-16

*What is your beloved more than
 another beloved,
O fairest among women?
What is your beloved more than
 another beloved,
 that you thus adjure us?*

*My beloved is all radiant and ruddy,
 distinguished among ten thousand.
 His head is the finest gold;
  his locks are wavy,
  black as a raven.
 His eyes are like doves
 beside springs of water,
  bathed in milk,
  fitly set.
His cheeks are like beds of spices,
 yielding fragrance.
 His lips are lilies,
 distilling liquid myrrh.
His arms are rounded gold,
 set with jewels.
His body is ivory work,
 encrusted with sapphires.*

Day 5

> *His legs are alabaster columns,*
> *set upon bases of gold.*
> *His appearance is like Lebanon,*
> *choice as the cedars.*
> *His speech is most sweet,*
> *and he is altogether desirable.*
> *This is my beloved and this is my friend,*
> *O daughters of Jerusalem.*

THE QUESTION IS asked as to what is so special about the loved one. Such analysis is not necessarily something that we deliberately undertake. One who is loved is loved for more than their physical appearance, though in the Song of Songs, physicality is ever present. Today, our consciences are especially aware of not judging by the looks a person has, or the age, or the form, ethnicity, sex or dress. We are encouraged to avoid prejudice and stereotyping another, yet this becomes ever easier the more open we are to another. Familiarity, far from breeding contempt in this situation, brings the deeper issues of personality, compassion and individual recognition to bear. We can see ourselves in and through another, and, indeed Christ in the eyes of another, all the better if we know them well. The apprehension of the kind of beautiful expression that the author is putting into words at the end of chapter 5 is helpful in its metaphors, for, read carefully, they are in no way comparing beauty of a particular kind, they are seeing beauty how the beauty is perceived.

Moments of Love

Let's look more closely. What does she mean in looking upon a man's legs as *alabaster columns set upon bases of gold*, or the whole body as, *ivory work encrusted with sapphires*? Yes, well, it is all rather cold though glorious – and nor would one wish to kiss lips dripping with *liquid myrrh*, however expensive. Surely what is being described here is an eye for opulence and splendour, rather than an outpouring of amorous attraction?

As I understand it, we have a disturbance in the outcome of love on this fifth day, in this fifth chapter of the Song of Songs. There is a stiltedness in the expression, and pain in desire being unfulfilled. The absence of the lover is bringing heartache, and the search has lost its joy, with questions raised and words spoken that have hurt; the lover is left wounded, imagining wondrous things and finding silence and loneliness, whilst describing in terms that capture the heights of beauty in the beloved being sought in a way that merely extenuates the feelings of being distanced and wounded.

What is it of the one you love that makes them, to you, more beloved than any other beloved? The question is asked twice and the answer given in chapter 5 is unsettling. It is a question for us to answer, both for our personal loves in this life, as it is to answer in the analogous desire for a deep love for Christ. *What is your beloved more than another beloved?*

This is not for us to overstrain tonight. This is not a request for an answer before we retire to bed. It is a thought to turn our minds and hearts from the wounding of love to its healing power; to rest in the peace of our Lord's presence, that the very reason why we are seeking and responding

Day 5

to the call of Christ is to have the bonds of coldness and rejection and abandonment – the sense of forsakenness – broken and love's restoring, renewing work allowed to happen. That is where our prayer takes us tonight. We look to the wounds of what love can bring us, and embrace its restoring, healing power, that is beyond anything else the source of all that is good and true in human nature and reflects the divine within us.

PRAYER

Loving Father,
look in your mercy upon me tonight.
Grant me peace and a restful night,
not because I am without the wounds of love,
within me or within those I see in the world
    around me,
or hold as the treasure of my heart,
but because I am yours and I give myself
to that commitment this night and always.
Bless those I love both in this life
and those in your nearer presence, eternally,
in Christ Jesus my Lord.
Amen.

DAY 6
Seeing

DAY 6
Morning

Song of Songs 6:1-3

> *Where has your beloved gone,*
> *O fairest among women?*
> *Which way has your beloved turned,*
> *that we may seek him with you?*
>
> *My beloved has gone down to his garden,*
> *to the beds of spices,*
> *to pasture his flock in the gardens,*
> *and to gather lilies.*
> *I am my beloved's and my beloved is mine;*
> *he pastures his flock among the lilies.*

IN THE PAST five days we have felt the welcome and acceptance that is at some stage in our Christian lives the opening that recognises that mercy, love and forgiveness are the overwhelming expressions of knowing ourselves, in a vital sense, to be 'at home'. In response, our searching for how to achieve a closer walk with God leads us to observe beauty with fresh eyes, or maybe eyes that are truly opened for the first time, at least in a spiritual sense. The discovery that love make us vulnerable as well as alive is an aspect of growth in grace that (with other noble aspirations) is shared by many of other religious traditions and none. Today we look beyond beauty to see what we need to see, what we must avoid turning our eyes from, if we are to truly embrace and hold fast the way of discipleship; the way of the Cross.

This morning the question is, 'To where has the beloved gone?' The beloved has turned from the path and gone to his garden. The verses end with the observation that, *I am my beloved's and my beloved is mine*. Following on from yesterday's feelings of abandonment and consequently suffering the wound of love, there is a reassertion of the mutual possession that the lovers hold. This underpins the very life of love, and brings healing in time of injury.

The lover follows the beloved with eyes opened to his turning away and finding solace in the garden of his delights, among the beds of spices and amongst the flocks pastured with lilies. Though we may have a picture in our minds here of lambs grazing amongst the white lilies of Easter, more likely are the 'lilies of the field' being lilies of the pasture, which is probably a collective name being used here for the flowers that bloom during the spring exuberance of grasses and brightly-coloured daisy-like flowers of the countryside, including the 'lily' or crown anemone (*Anemone coronaria*).

There is a deepening understanding of the lover being reflected here, as she, having lived through a wounding, finds restoration and renewed conviction in oneness of purpose and relationship, *I am my beloved's and my beloved is mine*.

The seeking is being shared; the looking has been assumed by those who care for the woman,

Day 6

encouraging her, as the Christian is not alone, but works through questioning, and their personal pilgrimage of faith, within a Church family and amongst friends. It has been said that lovers meet at Calvary,[18] and within this searching amongst those wounded, one can see the sense of this comment, at the point of the contemplation of the wounds of Christ. We also know that near Golgotha there was a garden, and in a further turn of the allegory, Christ's body was laid in the bed of the garden tomb having been wrapped in linen with a great weight of spices; *I am my beloved's and my beloved is mine*.

PRAYER

Father,
at the foot of your Son's cross,
we know that we are beloved.
Bring the sense of my sorrow for sin
with my need of forgiveness
to enhance my desire
to love as I am loved,
and live and show forth that love
in the world for which Christ died.
In his name I bring this prayer.
Amen.

---

[18] See further comment on this point tomorrow.

DAY 6
Midday

Song of Songs 6:4-10

*You are beautiful as Tirzah,[19] my love,
comely as Jerusalem,
terrible as an army with banners.
Turn away your eyes from me,
for they overwhelm me!
Your hair is like a flock of goats,
moving down the slopes of Gilead.
Your teeth are like a flock of ewes,
that have come up from the washing;
all of them bear twins,
and not one among them is bereaved.
Your cheeks are like halves of a pomegranate
behind your veil.
There are sixty queens and eighty concubines,
and maidens without number.
My dove, my perfect one, is the only one,
the darling of her mother,
flawless to her that bore her.
The maidens saw her and called her happy;
the queens and concubines also, and they
praised her.*

---

[19] Tirzah was once an important city in Israel during the period of the divided kingdom; cf. 1 Kings 15:21. Tirzah means 'the pleasant'.

Day 6

> *'Who is this that looks forth like the dawn,*
> *fair as the moon, bright as the sun,*
> *terrible as an army with banners?'*

THERE IS DEEP seeing in the words of this midday reading. Superficial beauty is seen with an inner realisation that finery can display power, splendour can declare superiority, awe tip over into fear. The wound of love has opened eyes as it has deepened understanding, that love is not surface deep, but that the real and eternal quality that St Paul described in his great hymn of love in 1st Corinthians chapter 13 overcomes because it is not blind, weak and capitulating, but clear-eyed and indestructible in the face of what attempts to destroy it.

The reading of the Song of Songs chapter 6 verses 4 to 10 brings the similes of the author to consider the likeness of the beloved woman to be special, as close to perfection, indeed, as can bear comparison to sixty queens and eighty concubines. There is no notion as to whether or not the woman in question would want her comparison to be made in such a way, or accept the intended admiration to fall in with eyes likened to newly washed goats and cheeks as half-pomegranates. Her perfection is linked with that of a dove, and underlined with the praise of her companions.

Teasing out the thread from yesterday unto

Moments of Love

this point today, we can see how the extension of love's exploration of relationship building has led through wounds, temporary absence, critical opinions and enticing comparisons. These have a very human feel to them. The deepening of love is facing the questionings and stripping back of real experience. Entering the second half of the Song of Songs, we find that love is bearing the testing of human fickleness, but at the same time sensing that such testing, though real and serious, is not damaging the underlying effect of love on the human soul faithful to the beloved, and known to be loved in his/her turn.

The Song of Songs, though with apparently no very clear literary structure, has a pattern (possibly showing itself entirely inadvertently) demonstrating a progression of thought; a thread which I am following, drawn out of the text, without it being necessarily a deliberate device of the author. The last verse (verse 10) of this section, for example, could be taken as the first verse of the next passage, but it fits better here, as a veiled enticement, or cryptic invitation to the lover to come with her amongst the fields and fruit of the open country. On the back of the fine descriptions of her perfection in his eyes we have this response of delight and desire. The restoration after injury, loneliness, coldness and the taunting of others is about to be celebrated in a return to the beauty of all that lies about them.

Day 6

PRAYER

Lord Jesus,
when you search for me,
as for a sheep gone astray,
I know that feeling of being special
though I deserve nothing and
am aware of every frailty I possess.
In the light of your presence,
and the invitation to follow,
grant me the grace to accept,
and the faith to be constant,
to you this day and forever.
Amen.

DAY 6
Evening

Song of Songs 6:11-12

> *I went down to the nut orchard,*
> *to look at the blossoms of the valley,*
> *to see whether the vines had budded,*
> *whether the pomegranates were in bloom.*
> *Before I was aware, my fancy set me*
>   *in a chariot beside my prince.*

THE INVITATION FROM one lover to the other we heard earlier today, and their meeting once more is within the fruitful fields, orchards and vineyards of the countryside. Of the three likely nuts (almonds, walnuts and pistachios) it is likely that the orchard was of walnuts. Dr David Darom, an Israeli marine biologist, living in Jerusalem, who has also studied and photographed the plants of the Holy Land for many years writes:

'Walnuts once grew in abundance in the Holy Land, while the pistachio trees were introduced into the area from the East. The most common today, growing wild all over Israel, is the Almond. The wild almond is a bitter-seeded medium-sized tree that sheds its leaves at the beginning of winter. Later, it is the first to sprout into magnificent

Day 6

pink and white blossoms – before leaf setting – at the end of a cold winter. the sweet-seeded almond has been cultivated in the Holy Land for thousands of years, being grafted on the local wild bitter-seeded strains.'[20] On the basis that where almonds and pistachios are mentioned in the Bible (e.g., Numbers 17:8; Ecclesiastes 12:5; Genesis 43:11) they are named as such, the nuts of the Song of Songs 6:11 are probably walnuts (*Juglans regia*).

The words of verses 11 and 12 of chapter 6 indicate spring, with all the fruiting trees in blossom. The picture is of the lovers standing in a walnut grove overlooking a valley filled with the white and pink flowers of the fruit trees, and we can imagine this scene in all its early freshness and beauty. The restorative quality of nature, of which rediscovery has been made in our own day, is reflective of the times of lockdown during the COVID-19 pandemic, to the daily reminders through changes in world weather patterns of the damage to nature of which humanity is still guilty. There is a poignancy in the images in these verses, and a reminder too, that for all the tree-planting, allotment tending, renewable energy-generating and re-wilding of the twenty-first century, there is ever more to contemplate of our relationship with Creation, and subsequent response.

Our love for God has ever been close to our love for the world of his creation, and from the Garden of Gethsemane to the Garden of the

---

[20] *Beautiful Plants of the Bible: From the Hyssop to the Mighty Cedar Trees*, David Darom (Herzlia, Palphot Ltd.) p. 36.

Moments of Love

Resurrection, we have imagined Christ at prayer amongst the olive trees and risen and greeting Mary Magdalene at the tomb amidst the spring flowers of an April dawn. In these two verses of the Song of Songs we may thread our own expressions of moments of inspiration when out in God's world and ponder our memories of loving encounter.

Whilst we cannot simply dwell in imagination, when the reality of life so seriously affects us all, or if it doesn't it should, considering the state of human existence in this and every age, nevertheless neither do we turn from what is a gift without price for everyone, with the eyes to see the glory of divine love expressed in the miracle of life, from the tiniest and most primitive form of organism to the mighty whales and colossal trees, the intricate beauty of flowers and the flutter of the most delicate insect or bird.

The lovers leave in a chariot. The healing of the moment, as relationship is restored and we feel the fresh start in a more mature and understanding nature of the love that binds them. Let us embrace that restoration and love as evening falls and we rest before night.

PRAYER

Heavenly Father,
bring to me this evening
some feeling for the restorative
power of your creation.

Day 6

Let me touch and know,
hear and see,
what is about me.
Give me gratitude and the humility
to live ever thankful of your mercy,
through Jesus Christ my Lord.
Amen.

DAY 6
Night

Song of Songs 6:13

> *Return, return, O Shulammite!*
> *Return, return, that we may look upon you.*
>
> *Why should you look upon the Shulammite,*
> *as upon a dance before two armies?*

THE SHULAMMITE, MEANING either 'woman of Jerusalem', or 'peaceful one', is the name given here to the representative figure of the woman in the Song of Songs, and can be taken as one of the most positive reflections of a young woman in the Old Testament, as we have seen throughout the whole of the Song of Songs. Various suggestions have been given as to the relationship of this woman with Solomon. Perhaps we may take it as even 'the bride of Solomon'. Some consider Shulammite to be a derivation of Shunammite (i.e., a woman from Shunem, a village in the north of the country).

However that matter is resolved, we have another to consider in the 'dance before two armies', or 'dance of Mahanaim' as it is given in another form. Mahanaim is the place of the meeting of two armies or hosts. It is linked with

Day 6

the area east of the Jordan river, near the Jabbock, where Jacob and Esau met and were reconciled, prior to which Jacob wrestled with an angel. This is all a bit vague, but we can tease out of the unknowns of this verse 13 the themes of meeting and restoration, of peace and relationship which conclude a chapter of the Song of Songs that has been emotionally carrying us through some turmoil into a time of renewal and hope. We may look; we may dance. Love, if made ragged a little through loneliness, and wonder and taunts, has been reasserted in its underlying themes of faithfulness and truth. There is much that has been superficially disturbed that is now restored, and the message going into chapter 7 is carried in the glance of love and the dance of joy.

PRAYER

Father
as I settle to sleep this night,
grant me your peace and loving presence.
Surround me with your protection,
and bless me with renewed conviction
to live my life committed to loving you
above all, and my neighbour as myself.
May my eyes rest on, and my heart dance
   with joy for,
all that Jesus is to me, tonight and always.
Amen.

DAY 7
The Invitation of Love

DAY 7
Morning

Song of Songs 7:1-5

> *How graceful are your feet in sandals,*
> *O queenly maiden!*
> *Your rounded thighs are like jewels,*
> *the work of a master hand.*
> *Your navel is a rounded bowl*
> *that never lacks mixed wine.*
> *Your belly is a heap of wheat,*
> *encircled with lilies.*
> *Your two breasts are like two fawns,*
> *twins of a gazelle.*
> *Your neck is like an ivory tower.*
> *Your eyes are pools in Heshbon,*
> *by the gate of Bath-rabbim.*
> *Your nose is like a tower of Lebanon,*
> *overlooking Damascus.*
> *Your head crowns you like Carmel,*
> *and your flowing locks are like purple;*
> *a king is held captive in the tresses.*

THE OPENING VERSES of chapter seven remind us of the first seven verses of chapter four. The lover is describing how his beloved is entrancing him, in a way that indicates his passion is by no means abated by the times of separation and loneliness that both have endured with the taunting of the onlookers. The maturing in love is for us assumed, and that this is more than a mere recapitulation of the earlier words of desire and commitment.

Looking at some of the specific references, within these expressions of desire, *Your eyes are pools in Heshbon, by the gate of Bath-rabbim* is one worthy of note. Probably this is a reference to a fish pool and to the sparkling water and glimmer of fish seen in the clear water beside the city of Heshbon some fifty miles east of Jerusalem and lying, as with the Jabbock and Mahanaim earlier today, in the Kingdom of Jordan. Heshbon is mentioned many times in the Old Testament. Originally a Moabite city but held by Solomon in the extent of the widening territory of his reign, it was a place of peace and refuge and a beautiful and secure city. It is known from archaeological excavations in the area that there were deep pools in the region, and so the references in this opening part of chapter 7 and from the end of chapter 6 are indicating contemplation of still, deep, peace, beauty, security and strength.

Then from the sparkling waters of a lake the images pass to the heights: a tower in Lebanon, a Syrian hill overlooking Damascus, and Mount Carmel standing sentinel over the Mediterranean Sea. From the dweller on the mountaintop to the one contemplating the still waters of a pool, the essence of beauty is captured with grandeur and expansive metaphor. This is no passing attraction; this is a longing for the most intimate and permanent of relationships.

As we take this within ourselves and read over the descriptions of thighs, navel, belly, breasts, neck eyes and nose, the head crowned with flowing locks

Day 7

of hair, we are in no doubt of the reality of the attraction within this relationship. How this can be allegorically adapted to imagine our own developing desire to be in closer communion with Christ Jesus, is best contemplated from the pools and the mountains. They ring especially significantly in the hearts and minds of those who are much affected by natural beauty in all its forms. Accepting that the Song of Songs is going to highlight the physical attractions of one human being for another, and within that ardent desire and arousal to reflect an adoration for God, we may feel some discomfort – or maybe not. That is for each to decide, in the intimacy of their own prayerful reflection. However, to stand on the heights and observe a view, or rest by a dazzling sunlit pool is nothing but a reason to slow one's pace and dream of how one might offer oneself in humility and love, to one who can sweep us up in the mystery of human relationships and the beauty of the natural world.

PRAYER

Father,
I stand at the side of a deep pool
and contemplate your love for me.
I stand upon a mountaintop
and feel very small.
Grant me this day, that lies before me
a vision of your glory
that draws me closer to
Jesus, Lord of my life.
Amen.

DAY 7
Midday

Song of Songs 7:6-9

How fair and pleasant you are,
O loved one, delectable maiden!
You are stately as a palm tree,
and your breasts are like its clusters.
I say I will climb the palm tree
and lay hold of its branches.
O may your breasts be like clusters of the vine,
and the scent of your breath like apples,
and your kisses like the best wine
that goes down smoothly,
gliding over lips and teeth.

THE PHYSICALITY OF the desire expressed in these verses continues the lover's longing from earlier in the chapter, and from the beginning of our day. We left our thoughts this morning with the contemplation of what is lovely from the heights of the mountains and in the stillness of a pool. Now the picture changes from the blossoms of spring from chapter 6 to the imaginative signs of the fruitfulness of late summer and autumn at this point in chapter 7: clusters of dates on the palms, clusters of grapes on the vine; the scent of ripe apples and the taste of fine wine. The lusciousness of these things feeds

Day 7

the meditations on the physical desire of the lover for the one he loves.

In spiritual terms, allegorically speaking, let us be a little more analytical here. On the one hand, one could claim, quite simply, that all that is being said here is underlining the main theme of the Song of Songs. On the other hand, we have the need to see both the distant scene and the intimate desire to have parallels in the development of humanity's relationship with the divine, and not just an individual and their God, but a worshipping community being faithful and growing in outward unity and inward grace to serve and follow with integrity and commitment.

Evelyn Underhill, a prayerful and contemplative writer of the first half of the last century, spoke helpfully of the 'Double action of the soul, standing away from the Perfect in contemplation and seeking union with It in love.' She would understand the view from the heights and across the still pool, with the intimacy of the climbing for a cluster of dates or being moved by the scent of a freshly picked apple. She continued, describing, 'this double consciousness of the Holy as both Home and our Father', and that this is characteristic of, 'a fully developed Christian spirituality'.[21]

As we read the Song of Songs in a Christian context, we find in the imagery both disturbingly intimate pictures, with which it is not always easy to relate, but also a parallel with classical devotional and contemplative understanding that is quite in tune with the teaching of the saints on prayer. Evelyn Underhill provides us with another corrective, by stating that the intimate and the

[21] *Lent with Evelyn Underhill*, G.P. Mellick Belshaw, ed. (Mowbrays, 1964), p. 95.

transcendent, 'characters are not found in their classic completeness in any one individual'. Going on, she adds, 'We only discern their balanced splendour in the corporate life of surrendered spirits; the Communion of Saints. Not the individual mystic in his solitude, but the whole of that Mystical Body, in its ceaseless self-offering to God, is the unit of humanity in which we can find reflected the pattern of the spiritual life.'[22]

We are sensing a broadening of the terms of the loving relationship between God and humanity. From our individual quest for greater union with Christ, comes the parallel and connected embrace of the communion of saints in time and eternity – the Eucharistic fellowship of love that is never ending and eternally blessed in Christ.

PRAYER

Lord Jesus,
On the night that you were betrayed
and your followers were scattered,
you brought a deeper unity of love and fellowship
to those you had called to be with you.
They were frail and made mistakes,
as I am and do today.
Teach me the way to go on
that I may serve you and respond to your love
    for me,
in the fellowship of the Holy Spirit.
Amen.

[22] Ibid.

DAY 7
Evening

Song of Songs 7:10-12

> *I am my beloved's,*
> *and his desire is for me.*
> *Come, my beloved,*
> *let us go forth into the fields,*
> *and lodge in the villages;*
> *let us go out early to the vineyards,*
> *and see whether the vines have budded,*
> *whether the grape blossoms have opened*
> *and the pomegranates are in bloom.*
> *There I will give you my love.*

AS OUR RETREAT opened wider with the noontime reflection today, it is good to read Evelyn Underhill's words, reminding us that both transcendence and intimacy in relationships affect both divine and human bonds of love. Verses 10 to 12 of chapter 7 of the Song of Songs bring a fulfilment to the union of bride and bridegroom. There is a place found, where the vines are budding in the vineyard; where the pomegranates are in blossom. There is a time. There is a place. The meeting of the lovers is discovered.

Where might our meeting take place? Most

Moments of Love

likely our response will be at the place where we are accustomed to share the bread and wine in thanksgiving for the offering of Christ in love for the redemption of the world. We would, of course, be correct in this thought, both theologically and prayerfully. The mystery of the effect of what Jesus instituted at the Last Supper is beyond rational analysis. It is of the spirit and soul of Christian unity and shared remembrance, and experienced through faith, and we are taken back to the foot of the Cross.

Gilbert Shaw's *A Pilgrim Book of Prayers* speaks of Calvary as the 'meeting place of lovers'. This rings very true to our reading of the Song of Songs, as we interpret it in a Christian context. The words of Shaw's view of the Love shining from the Cross, come in a meditation on Calvary, under the title, *The consideration and composition of place*:

Calvary is not only a place and an occasion in history, but it is a spiritual reality in all times and places; for it is the at-one-ment of every soul to God.

It is in Calvary, the Blood-shedding of the Lamb, that Love in sacrifice draws out our love to the fullest possibility of our sacrifice of self to him.

It is there that the soul can come to know its depth – of sin, of nothingness and of possibility for God.

It is there, face to face with Love in action, that the soul can learn to make answer to his love.

It is the meeting place of lovers.[23]

---

[23] *A Pilgrim's Book of Prayers*, Gilbert Shaw (Mowbray, 1945; new edition SLG Press 1992), p. 67.

Day 7

Place is significant for both personal and corporate reasons. How easy it is to deny Christians their place on the principle of the Church being universal and a fellowship of believers, yet time and again the reality is that from the corner of the most crowded space to the vast areas of cathedrals and in the natural world of beaches, mountains and forests, the place of prayer and encounter with God is proven to be important.

The lovers go to the fields, the villages, the vineyards, and, whilst desire is not heightened, or even proven to be real because of such places, they are integral in the experience of these two lovers and in the experience of many a Christian soul and her or his God. As day seven of this retreat moves into the evening and the penultimate one of this time away, in mind and spirit, if not in body, let us ponder how important, or otherwise, the physical constraints of this retreat have proven to be. Have you sought a particular space? Have you needed a place to pray, to be silent, to consider the words and thoughts flowing from them as together we contemplate the Song of Songs and its context?

PRAYER

Heavenly Father,
Where my treasure is,
there my heart is also,
but where is that place?
Grant my Lord, the eyes to see

Moments of Love

and the imagination to understand
that in seeking I will find,
no matter where I make my own,
there you will be, and there
my life lies prostrate at Calvary
and renewed with Mary
at the empty tomb,
both, the meeting place of love
and of hope and faith and trust,
in your Son, Jesus Christ.
Amen.

DAY 7
Night

Song of Songs 7:13

> *The mandrakes give forth fragrance,*
> *and over our doors are all choice fruits,*
> *new as well as old,*
> *which I have laid up for you, O my beloved.*

THE FRAGRANCE OF the mandrake is said to be like that of an apple, and the intimation here is that it is heightening desire and intimacy. There is a comforting thought as we end this day that the easing into sleep is extenuated by fragrance and affinity as the scent of stored ripe fruit and freshly harvested fruit together bring a pleasing odour to our bedtime rest.

In prayer, being relaxed and at ease with a mind stilled with a candle burning or with scented oils and flowers, is an image which is often used today, with whole shops filled with every natural fragrance and plenty of imagined ones, too. But there is no doubt that within the commercial production of such aids to tranquillity and reflection there is a solid basis of experience that continues to attract those who find such help effective and soothing.

The need to be totally at ease tonight is also a way of countering the thought that, 'My retreat is over tomorrow'. It is too early to allow the distractions of the coming days or responsibility and commitments to intrude into the last twenty-four hours. These can be amongst the most vital hours of our withdrawal, and so lay thoughts of what is to come to one side, and concentrate on the needful: the rest and peace of this moment. Consider the lovers in their bower, the fragrant fruits and the hideaway with Christ; however you may envisage your intimacy in prayer can be expressed. Your space, be it only your chair or your bed, is a place special to you and in a way holy to this retreat.

PRAYER

> Lord Jesus,
> as the candle flame flickers,
> bringing soft light that burns
> into the dark hours of this night,
> let me rest in you, and
> should unease or anxiety of any kind
> assault me in the coming night,
> that your abiding presence
> may restore in me a sense of the peace
> that passes my understanding,
> and your gift that I may never lose.
> Amen.

DAY 8
Consummation

DAY 8
Morning

Song of Songs 8:1-4

*O that you were like a brother to me,
who nursed at my mother's breast!
If I met you outside, I would kiss you,
and no one would despise me.
I would lead you and bring you
into the house of my mother,
and into the chamber of the one who bore me.
I would give you spiced wine to drink,
the juice of my pomegranates.
O that his left hand were under my head,
and that his right hand embraced me!
I adjure you, O daughters of Jerusalem,
do not stir up or awaken love
until it is ready!*

THE MIND IS cast back, or thoughts linked to the past places of love and intimacy. Nothing is hurried, the awakening of love will take its own time, the relationship of wife and husband may echo the closeness of that of brother or mother. The sense of fulfilment is declared as the opportunity arises, and so on the final day of the retreat the theme of consummation is developed on lines of past remembrance and relationship opening the occasion for present joy.

I am reminded of an unforgettable poem by Denise Levertov. She recalls a moment of supreme illumination as a child in her poem *First Love*. In it she describes an experience that she had as a very young child, the effects of which she lived with ever after. I quote the whole poem as it is needed for its full impact and understanding:

First Love

It was a flower.

There had been,
before I could even speak,
another infant, girl or boy unknown,
who drew me – I had
an obscure desire to become
connected in some way to this other,
even to *be* what I faltered after, falling
to hands and knees, crawling
a foot or two, clambering
up to follow further until
arms swooped down to bear me away.
But that one left no face, had exchanged
no gaze with me.

This flower:
        suddenly
there was *Before I saw it,* the vague
past, and *Now.* Forever. Nearby
was the sandy sweep of the Roman Road,
and where we sat the grass
was thin. From a bare patch
of that poor soil, solitary,

Day 8

> sprang the flower, face upturned.
> looking completely, openly
> into my eyes.
>   I was barely
> old enough to ask and repeat its name.
>
> 'Convolvulus', said my mother:
> Pale shell-pink, a chalice
> no wider across than a silver sixpence.
>
> It looked at me, I looked
> back, delight
> filled me as if
> I, not the flower,
> were a flower and were brimful of rain.
> *And there was endlessness.*
> Perhaps through a lifetime what I've desired
> has always been to return
> to that endless giving and receiving, the
> wholeness
> of that attention,
> that once-in-a-lifetime
> secret communion.[24]

Moments of intense intimacy with a vision that is responding to something – in fact, ultimately, someone – beyond ourselves leaves a lasting impression. Maybe not on the scale of Denise Levertov's eye-opening epiphany, but still of sufficient merit to demand thought years later, and be a reminder, if life has left us hardened and insensitive to what is most delicate and transient in the world around us, that we need

---

[24] *New Selected Poems*, Denise Levertov (Bloodaxe Books, 2003), p.195.

to regain lost sight in patience, slowing the pace of reflection, prayer and our desire to achieve as time apparently is running out.

This is a voice that needs to be heard at the end of a retreat that brings light and life to the lovely things of this mortal existence. In understanding the transient, we come to understand more of the eternal. A convolvulus flower is amongst the shortest-lived of blooms. They come and go in a few hours and yet, as they cup the raindrops and look upward at a child's delighted face, the whole world of wonder unfolds for a toddler. My own grandchildren have taught me once more to own the experiences of wonder and accept the moments of joy thankfully as they appear even to those approaching or beyond their three-score years and ten.

Take a moment this morning to recall an instant in your own life, or seek in slow appreciation of what is around you to see further into something you may have only given a glance to before.

PRAYER

Dear Lord,
May my head rest on your left hand
my body to be held with your right.
In loving fellowship with the whole Church,
here and in eternity,
may pain and sorrow and the anguish of the
    bereaved
know the holding embrace of your presence.

Day 8

Bring healing of memories, sad times and hurts,
as love draws relations and friends,
and locates within the experience of each one,
something of the wonder and vision
of the young child, still within the heart
of each one who turns to you in faith and
  desire,
to be held and go forth in the inspiration
of the Holy Spirit in whom I pray.
Amen.

DAY 8
Midday

Song of Songs 8:5-7

*Who is that coming up from the wilderness,
leaning upon her beloved?*

*Under the apple tree I awakened you.
There your mother was in labour with you;
there she who bore you was in labour.*

*Set me as a seal upon your heart,
as a seal upon your arm;
for love is strong as death,
passion fierce as the grave.
Its flashes are flashes of fire,
a raging flame.
Many waters cannot quench love,
neither can floods drown it.
If one offered for love
all the wealth of one's house,
it would be utterly scorned.*

IN THE MIDDLE OF the last day of this retreat we read the best known of all lines in the Song of Songs. Verses 6 and 7 have become known as they are used as a canticle in some Christian traditions,

Day 8

and will slip off the tongue of those who know and use it often, especially in Passiontide. They are a form of drawing together of the threads of this retreat too, as the strength of love in the face of what is potentially life transforming, through death or disaster or accumulation of wealth. Love stands beyond these things and is untouched by them. That we can understand. Anyone who has stood at a graveside, or within the congregation at a funeral, and has heard a parent, spouse, grandchild, daughter or son, or close friend talk of the one they love, will recognise that, *love is strong as death, passion fierce as the grave.* Disaster, such as brought about by a flood, cannot destroy love, and money is scorned in the face of love. These two verses sum up the whole poem that is the Song of Songs.

This midday reading begins with location once more, but before we get to that place of encounter, let us recap the steps that have guided our thoughts in the past week. As we began our retreat the joy of knowing we were received, drawn in, comforted and loved was a primary experience. Coming from days when we were less attentive and were bound up in other matters, to know and be embraced by the loving presence of Christ is the emotion that launches desire from the receiving end. The first two days are passive and gave us a pause for thought as to how and when to express the desire of our hearts for something more; something active in grasping and responding to the love of God in Christ Jesus.

The quest is a response that echoes the parables of Luke 15, as the search for a sheep, a coin and a son are themselves reflections on a theme, but for the Song of Songs, beauty is never

Moments of Love

far from the exposure to love, and in life and its desires, through the experience of much ugliness that is an essential part of life too, the beauty of God is reflected in the beauty that we encounter through the senses which are our joy to possess.

The second half of the week brings us to own that, 'no man is an island, complete unto himself'[25], but love is experienced in relationship, and not all relationships are perfect, and even those that are near perfection will be tested, with wounds and questions, misunderstandings and grief. Love does not exist in isolation, nor can we protect ourselves from injury. Rather the very opposite. Those who seek to lose their life gain it and those who try to hold it to themselves, lose it. This we know and understand from living life, as we recognise the healing nature of love in even the most extreme of circumstances. In fact the more extreme the situation, the more amazing the love. This has brought us to the place of meeting, and this midday it brings us to the place of birth, the creation of new life, the acknowledgement of a fresh start; as with John the Baptist and Jesus, one declines as the other ascends. It is of the nature of human existence and in love encapsulates the freedom of life's gift.

The choice of the apple tree under which love was kindled, was awoken, is interesting. The tree that in the Garden of Eden was presented as an allegorical picture of the source of the knowledge of good and evil, is here used in a different way, reflective of fruitfulness as opposed to the

---

[25] The quote is from 'Meditation XVII' by John Donne through which he explores the connectedness of humanity in life and in death.

Day 8

withered remains of what had been good and has now become wasted, here the reminder is of birth and fulfilment and completion. At this point, the indestructibility of love is honoured and extolled.

PRAYER

Father,
into your loving presence I commit myself
 today.
Through all the ups and downs of my life,
help me remember to see each day
as a microcosm of life itself,
and each loving experience
as a fraction of all the love I own,
in and through you and your Son,
Jesus Christ my Lord.
Amen.

DAY 8
Evening

Song of Songs 8:8-12

> *We have a little sister,*
> *and she has no breasts.*
> *What shall we do for our sister,*
> *on the day when she is spoken for?*
> *If she is a wall,*
> *we will build upon her a battlement of silver;*
> *but if she is a door,*
> *we will enclose her with boards of cedar.*
> *I was a wall,*
> *and my breasts were like towers;*
> *then I was in his eyes*
> *as one who brings peace.*
> *Solomon had a vineyard at Baal-hamon;*
> *he entrusted the vineyard to keepers;*
> *each one was to bring for its fruit a thousand*
> *pieces of silver.*
> *My vineyard, my very own, is for myself;*
> *you, O Solomon, may have the thousand,*
> *and the keepers of the fruit two hundred!*

THE PROTECTION OF the young is amongst the most pressing human desires. Where love is shared, the need to protect is even more urgent.

Day 8

Unknown children are still precious, our own young family members are most of all. As we continue to dwell on what love can bear within us, the author of the Song of Songs is describing the striving for safety of those who can protect the loved ones of the lovers. We may attempt to build walls of security with whatever resources we have, and enclose within such a metaphorical building one for whom our love is greater than for our life itself, but, in fact, we all must rely on others for the safety of those closest to us, release, as we must, children and grandchildren to become themselves and grow into what God intends them to become, and know that the shield of love is the ultimate bond, but can never be an insurance against hurt.

The example of Solomon's vineyard at Baal-hamon demonstrates the point. There is a share in its profits and its fruit, but, it remains, his, 'very own'. There is an inevitable uneasiness about this discussion on security and possession. It is a conundrum which will resolve itself as we settle to sleep later, but the thread of its reasoning from the vulnerable child to the trusted keeper, wreathed in anxiety for those ultimately responsible and utterly absorbed in love, is an entrance to prayer. Step onto that place and open for the sake of all whom you love, the heartfelt prayer for those you care for but cannot and should not surround in the cotton wool of absolute protection.

These are verses that release us from the burden of absolute care. That lies with the Father. When we have done all we can for those we love, we can do no more. Our prayer for life is the prayer of love; our desire to give is the desire of love; but we learn to release those we love as we learn to let go of the life we have within us and which we express as we live it.

PRAYER

Heavenly Father,
in love I hold those I name in my heart
 before you.
Guide and protect those dear to me,
and give me the sense to know when to let
 go
and when to cling on, when is the moment
when I need to shed responsibility,
and how I should do it in and through the
 love
that we share, and which is beyond price,
and eternal,
in and through that love that you show to
 me
in the death and resurrection of your Son,
Jesus Christ my Lord.
Amen.

DAY 8
Night

Song of Songs 8:13-14

> *O you who dwell in the gardens,*
> *my companions are listening for your voice;*
> *let me hear it.*
>
> *Make haste, my beloved,*
> *and be like a gazelle*
> *or a young stag*
> *upon the mountains of spices!*

LYING DOWN TONIGHT thankful of these eight days of abiding, let any tension ebb and flow, sleep come in quiet and peaceful rest, stillness reflect the loving presence of he who dwells within. May listening be the activity of your body, and the only haste that of commitment in love to the one who calls. From these days, the Song of Songs has given in image and energy, none of which will be lost in the days of activity to come.

As this retreat ends, may the eternity of love renewed in knowledge and understanding be what carries us in the hours and days and months to come. Where determination and intent are galvanising you to something new and fresh, or maybe to a further period of inactivity and reflection, may the Lord Jesus Christ be the truth that leads you into the place of your dwelling, in heart and mind and body.

As the spirit lights and refreshes us for what is before us, may your heart be as a gazelle and your inspiration lifted with the scent of the beautiful things of this world and the anticipation of our final consummation in love in the age to come. Be blessed tonight and in the quiet solitude of your thoughts and prayers, find a peace which is an intent to hear the voice of him who loves you, and always will.

PRAYER

Lord, protect me this night,
in silent hours, in sleep and in waking,
may your holy angels be a guard around my bed,
your presence lift me, unconsciously to a deeper
appreciation and understanding of your love,
for me, and all those I love in and through you,
Amen.